Mind Matters

Mind Matters

A RESOURCE GUIDE TO PSYCHIATRY FOR BLACK COMMUNITIES

Christina,
Thanks for all
the support over the
years. You have truly been
a friend! Continue to do great
work + break down more barriers
w/ mental illness! Jeff

Global Health Psychiatry

ISBN-13: 9781979510684
ISBN-10: 1979510687
Library of Congress Control Number: 2018903729
CreateSpace Independent Publishing Platform
North Charleston, South Carolina

This book is dedicated to the parents, families, mentors, elders, teachers, colleagues, classmates, communities of friends, and church families who supported this group of doctors along the way. As the African proverb says, "It takes a village to raise a child." The doctors who have written this book are the products of those villages. We take it as an honor to dedicate this book to you.

Media, Speaking Engagements, Booking, and Contact Information

---

Global Health Psychiatry
Website: GHPsychiatry.com
E-mail: info@GHPsychiatry.com
Facebook/Instagram/LinkedIn/Twitter: @GHPsychiatry

Contents

Preface

Does Black Mental Health Actually Matter?

Culture and Race in America

This book specifically focuses on the mental health needs of African Americans. African Americans have a unique place in American history due to the transatlantic slave trade that occurred over four hundred years, displacing millions of Africans to the Americas. African Americans, also referred to as black Americans, currently total over forty million who are descendants of the transatlantic slave trade. From the bondage of slavery, abolition, constitutional amendments, and the civil rights movement, blacks in America have only had rights and privileges as full citizens in the United States for fifty years, which is a little more than two generations. Even today we continue to see disparities in economics, jobs, health-care, education, pay, loans, business, and mental health care. That is not to say there have been no gains, but for many, the gains continue to be slow. The combined communities' continual effects of bondage for four hundred years, lack of full rights as citizens, and continual discrimination, racism, and belief that a group of people is inferior or superior due to expression of skin pigmentation continue to plague relationships throughout the country.

We are living in interesting times in America when it comes to race and culture. It seems as if we are dealing with old demons that we thought we buried in the past with previous civil rights initiatives that were to protect all Americans. We are in the midst of anger, distrust, and questions about the directions the country is taking regarding the diversity for which the nation stands. Even though we are in a constant battle for "a more perfect union," we are still a nation of different backgrounds. Even though this is what makes America unique and great, it also causes points of contention, distrust, and anger, often turning us against one another. Regardless, this is a beautiful country and concept—that anyone can be great—but in recognizing this, we still have to understand that there are marginalized groups according to race, gender, class, socioeconomics, impoverishment, and sexual and gender identification.

Although this book specifically targets African Americans and discusses race, the reader will find that the book is applicable across races. Racism, sexism, xenophobia, inequity, poverty, classism, religion, and nationalism are not specific to one group or culture in America. We should be able to recognize that there is only one race, and that is the human race, but instead we live in a culture of race where we willingly are or have been convinced that there are differences in race. Socially and culturally we are made to live in a society where we are forced to take race into account.

When understanding the mental health of blacks, it is important to understand the history and current issues that affect black Americans. These unique cultural and historic experiences cause variations in how we black Americans view and receive mental health treatment. This often directly influences their mental health and the perspectives they have on their own personal and mental well-being. By the end of this book, readers should better understand that black mental health matters and that cultural variabilities complicate and influence this historical and large minority group.

Acknowledgments

would truly like to express my sincerest thanks to the group of psychiatrists who agreed to help me with this project. I know that this entire team has very busy lives and active practices and that they are attempting to juggle many aspects of their lives while at the same time contributing to this book, struggling to make deadlines, and making personal sacrifices in order to complete this work. This is an assembly of friends as well as colleagues. We hope that you find this book useful for those who need mental health care.

The authors of this book are all psychiatrists of African descent. We share a common interest in the mental health of all patients and were brought together through our involvement with several psychiatric medical organizations, including the Black Psychiatrists of America, the psychiatry section of the National Medical Association, and the American Psychiatric Association. The authors have all worked both individually and collectively in promoting mental health in all populations but also have done work targeting the mental health of underserved populations. Much of this work has been specific to the needs of African Americans. The authors have all worked in diverse groups of practice settings, giving them unique insights into the needs of patients from multiple communities.

Together, we want to thank Ms. Marilyn King, former assistant program director of APA Minority Fellowship Program, and Dr. Annelle Primm, former APA deputy director. Your hard work and dedication directly led to the development of the authors of this book. We must also congratulate Dr. Altha Stewart on being the first black president-elect of the American Psychiatric Association.

We also would like to acknowledge the many mentors who have passed since the start of this project, all of whom dedicated their life's work to mental health and served as mentors to black psychiatrists and the black community and are sorely missed by all. The following list is brief and not all-encompassing, but all are dear to the work that helped produce this book.

As we were writing this book and formulating our ideas, we were thinking of all the mentors and great psychiatrists who influenced our careers and who have passed. These psychiatrists include Drs. Francis Cress Welsing, Chester Pierce, Harry Wright, Phyllis Harrison Ross, George Mallory, and Beny Primm, among many others. We cannot thank these pioneers, who are now ancestors, enough for their work and their contributions to the profession of psychiatry and those who carry on their tireless work.

—Napoleon B. Higgins Jr. MD

Introduction

The purpose of this book is to be a usable resource for individuals and families affected by mental illness. The book focuses on African American families due to the specific needs and issues of mental health in this population. These issues include disparities in care in most settings, cultural differences in how symptoms present, and concerns and common myths about illnesses that affect the mind. Although this book is specific to African American families, it is a usable resource for anyone who is, or family members of someone who is, affected by mental health. The information contained in this book crosses cultures, families, and race in that mental health is seen in all communities and may cause difficulties for patients and families who love them. We understand that mental illness and psychiatric disorders not only affect the individual suffering from the illness but also the family who loves and provides support for them. When one person suffers, the entire family is affected and suffers along with him or her. We hope that by the end of this book, the reader will understand how mental illness affects the individual, the family, the home, the extended family, and, collectively, the community.

The authors hope that this book will be a useful, easy-to-read resource that will serve as a mental health first aid kit for families. It is meant to be read from cover to cover as an educational tool in mental health or as individual chapters for a specific interest. Because each chapter is written to be independent of the others, it may seem to be repetitive on certain topics due to similarity between illnesses and symptoms being common to more than one mental health disorder.

There are many stigmas about what psychiatry means, and when needing services, people can have to deal with fear, embarrassment, jokes, teasing, and sincere concern. We hope that with this book, we can demystify the word *psychiatry* so that others can know that mental disorders are not something to fear or ridicule but can understand that these are medical disorders of the mind that are treatable so that patients do not needlessly suffer.

As psychiatrists, we can see the fear and anxiety of the patients sitting across from us. They often fear what the next hour of examination is going to discover; they fear what will be said, what will be revealed, or being told that they are "crazy." Patients also fear that the psychiatrist is judging them when they express their secrets and expose many of their most embarrassing moments. There is the fear of medications and how they will affect their minds and bodies. Will they get addicted, and how severely will it change their behavior?

This book is important now due to the current crisis of poor mental health education. We see continually on the news the issue of untreated mental health needs of people who suffer from a lack of access, care, and support. You also see the crisis of untreated mental illness, where acts of violence occur by people who are mentally ill, but most often people who are mentally ill are victims of violence and not vice versa. We are seeing shooting and killing of the mentally ill by the police and mentally ill people committing violent acts as well. Most often what occurs is an overwhelming problem due to a lack of information, causing ignorance about mental illness. This contributes to difficulties receiving care, lack of community resources, and poor reimbursement for physicians who provide care to this vulnerable population. Sadly, people suffer needlessly when there is proven help so that symptoms can be controlled in order to diminish the effect on the patient's family and life.

This book differs from any other that we know of collectively because it concentrates on patients, families, and caregivers. It is meant to be a usable guide to help patients, caregivers, communities, and people interested in mental health. Most often, books on psychiatry written by psychiatrists are meant specifically for psychiatrists. This book is written for the patients, families, community activists, social workers, police officers, paramedics, and first responders. It is a useful tool for individuals interested in mental health so that they can learn for themselves or take what they learn back to the community. It is written so that it can be understandable and easily digestible for patients' families and for just about anyone interested in mental health or psychiatry. We want the patient to feel empowered with knowledge to help decrease the fear of psychiatry, psychiatrists, psychiatric disorders, and people affected by mental health issues.

The framework of the book is to discuss the major psychiatric diagnoses that are most common. All diagnoses in this book are in reference to the *Diagnostic and Statistical Manual of Mental Disorders* (DSM-5) by the American Psychiatric Association.[1] Some names of mental health diagnoses are represented in a more conversational term by intention to better communicate to readers. It is not a comprehensive book of psychiatric disorders and will not cover all psychiatric illnesses that affect patients. The intent is to be a brief, usable book for the majority of patients. Also, we wanted to keep it short so that it can be easily referenced and not overwhelm the reader with information.

In this digital age, as psychiatrists we find that patients and the community will uncover some of the most outlandish ideas about psychiatry. We hope this book is a basic resource for where to start. It is designed to be read cover to cover, but readers will also be able to go to specific chapters that pertain to them as individuals. This book is useful for professionals who want to provide their patients with a resource for information about and understanding of their diagnoses and what to expect in treatment and care.

At times you will see the book use *African American* and *black* interchangeably. You will also see multiple terms for individuals who are receiving care from physicians; these include *patient, consumer, client,* individual names, and so on. This was left to the discretion of each writer.

Names and case studies in this book are fictitious. Any resemblance to real persons, living or dead, is purely coincidental. The information contained in these case studies are for educational use only.

—Napoleon B. Higgins Jr., MD

Note

1. American Psychiatric Association, *Diagnostic and Statistical Manual of Mental Disorders*, 5th ed. (Washington, DC: American Psychiatric Association, 2013).

CHAPTER 1

Overview: What Does a Psychiatrist Do?

NAPOLEON B. HIGGINS JR., MD

What is a psychiatrist?

A psychiatrist is a medical doctor who specializes in treating people with mental health disorders, including anxiety, depression, and issues with focus, attention, anger, substance abuse, and many other things.

How do psychiatrists diagnose patients?

Psychiatrists diagnose patients using the *Diagnostic and Statistical Manual of Mental Disorders (DSM-5)*. During the interview, the psychiatrist asks a set of questions to understand your reasons for seeking or being brought in for mental health care. From a combination of the initial complaints, the questions will help to get a better understanding of a patient's individual needs. There often will be other information used to make a diagnosis, such as how the person is behaving during the interview and/or gathering information from family members, school, work, or friends. This information must be gathered with consent from the patient. Exceptions include situations where the person being interviewed is a minor and has a parent or legal guardian. Also, there are often emergency situations when there is a need to protect the patient, who is intending to hurt himself or herself or who may cause others to react and hurt him or her. There are also exceptions if an individual is a threat to another individual or to the public.

After this information is gathered, the psychiatrist will decide if there is a mental health diagnosis to make according to *DSM-5* criteria. It is important to understand that not all mental health problems rise to the level of a diagnosable mental illness. Also understand that in order for it to be a psychiatric diagnosis, it must cause significant problems. The difficulty in functioning must cause an issue with not being able to go to work or school. Other impairments may include not being able to take care of oneself appropriately or not being able to handle life responsibilities, such as family or children.

When do you need to see a psychiatrist versus a psychologist, social worker, or pastoral counselor?

Psychiatrists are medical doctors who must go to medical school in order to practice medicine. We are trained in all medical disciplines, but we are doctors who do extra training specializing in mood and behavior. Mental health disorders are medical disorders that often need treatment by medical doctors. We often prescribe medications, but we also are trained to do therapy, counsel regarding illness, and understand other medical issues that may complicate mental functioning.

- Psychologists usually have a master's degree, PsyD, or PhD and do mostly therapy and psychological testing.
- Midlevel service providers often work with a psychiatrist or independently depending on individual state laws. Midlevel providers most often include physician assistants and psychiatric nurse practitioners who may have either a master's degree or PhD.
- Social workers are often used to find social services, such as places for treatment, resources for health care, housing, finances, and jobs or to provide therapy.

- Pastoral counseling is helpful for those who want a religious base to mental health care. Often mental health and religion are synonymous for many patients.

Realize that often combinations of multiple mental health providers are needed for optimal care.

Do mental health issues exist in the black community?

Race, culture, and color do not exclude a person from having a mental health condition. Too often when someone seeks a mental health professional, it is frequently the last resort or after having been made to go by family or school officials, or well too often it is after legal issues have occurred.

Do you have to be "crazy" to see a psychiatrist?

Most people do not realize how common mental health problems are. Approximately half of all adults and children will have a mental health disorder in their lifetimes. As many as one in five Americans will have a diagnosable mental disorder in one year. Most of these may not know there is an issue due to the brain not functioning correctly. This will cause many not to come in for help and to deny there is a problem. Many illnesses of the brain may be mild and manageable without requiring professional care. Some of the most common mental health issues are anxiety, depression, substance abuse, and additional issues that will be discussed further in upcoming chapters.

What is the role of religion in black mental health?

Many times blacks will consider mental health issues to be a failure in faith or not trusting in God. This causes mental health issues not to be seen as medical conditions but as questions of spirituality and faith. Many patients will have fatalistic thinking where depression or problems with the mind are punishment for past sins and behaviors rather than treatable mental health conditions. Some may believe that their sadness and suffering are part of being spoken to by God and a burden to bear as a badge for showing their connection to God due to feeling emotions so deeply. For some these thoughts and beliefs can be comforting, but for others it can prevent them from receiving the help they need.

Spirituality and religion are a significant source of strength for individuals and communities. Participants in religious services have shown to have improved mental health functioning. Church families can be extremely supportive to an individual or family affected by mental health. A sense of support and encouragement is helpful toward recovery. The church can also cause a group mental health dynamic where people are able to share stories and receive support from the group. Many churches have significant mental health services that include both trained mental health providers and supportive counseling services to laypeople, mentors, and elders.

For many it is impossible to separate mental health needs from spiritual needs. African Americans are more likely to be involved in organized religion, with 97 percent believing in God, 91 percent believing that religion is somewhat important to very important, 83 percent attending church regularly, and 73 percent praying daily. Oddly, psychiatrists are the least religious of all medical specialties and more likely than other doctors to not believe in God or organized religion. This causes a particular issue when the majority of African Americans believe in God and religion and the caregivers they are seeing do not. Even if the psychiatrist doesn't, he or she should be trained to understand the importance of religion and how it relates to a patient's individual needs. Because psychiatrists are born to an ethnicity, it would be assumed that black psychiatrists are more likely to believe in God, although there are no studies to cite.

Why is the family and community important to black mental health?

Frequently, modern psychiatry focuses on the individual and has less focus on the collective community in which the person lives. There is regularly a lot of interconnection between black family members and the community they live in when making health decisions. It is not only the individual who needs to understand the mental illness that is affecting him or her but also, and just as important, the individual's immediate family and greater community. A grandmother, a grandfather, another family member, or often an elder in the community or church could influence the final decision on treatment. The doctor may not realize that the individual will most likely discuss treatment with his or her extended family, and often the collective group will decide the next plan of action. This book's primary focus is on the individual's understanding of his or her mental health, and it is just as equally focused on the collective community in which the person lives. This book is written for those who are affected by, care for, and love those who are suffering from mental health issues.

CHAPTER 2

Depression

Don't We All Feel a Little Down Sometimes?
DELANE CASIANO, MD

Vivian is a thirty-five-year-old, divorced African American female who was referred by her primary care doctor to a women's mental health center. She arrived for the visit alone, neatly dressed and with a polite but hesitant approach toward the front desk staff. Although she appeared nervous at the start of the interview with the psychiatrist, she progressively appeared more relaxed as the discussion continued.

When asked how she was referred to the women's center, Vivian stated that she told her primary care doctor during her annual visit that she had been feeling "stressed out" for the past several months. Her primary care doctor told her that she had depression and referred her to the women's mental health center.

Depression: Doesn't everybody feel this way sometimes?

All individuals experience a range of emotions that vary from day to day or over the course of a lifetime. Numerous terms are used to describe emotions, such as *happy*, or a state of feeling joy or contentment; *angry*, or a strong feeling of being upset; and *afraid*, or fear that something bad will happen. Generally speaking, the term *depression* is used when a person is feeling sad or is in a state of feeling sorrow or unhappiness. In the field of psychiatry, the term *depression* is applied differently from the general public's use of the term. In this context, depression is a treatable medical condition during which individuals experience a change in mood as well as in the way they think, feel, and behave, ultimately causing distress or difficulty with living.

Upon further questioning by the psychiatrist, Vivian noted that she felt tired because she'd been having trouble sleeping and recently lost a few pounds because she hadn't had much of an appetite. She started to feel stressed out around the time she was placed on probation at her job a couple of months prior when she couldn't concentrate on her computer duties. She had been drinking a glass of wine in the evenings in order to "relax." Her primary care doctor recommended daily walks to help improve her energy, but she hadn't started yet because her motivation had been too low. In fact, she hadn't been interested in many of her usual activities either, noting that she hadn't return calls to her friends who had asked her to join them for lunch several times over the past month. She felt guilty about avoiding her friends as well as her troubles at work. She became tearful as the psychiatrist gently asked whether she ever felt hopeless or had thoughts about suicide. She stated that there were times when she thought about dying but cited her faith as a Christian as the reason she did not believe in suicide. She stated that she prayed often and went to Bible study and church, but nothing seemed to help. Her primary care doctor sent her for blood testing to see if she had any medical problems that could lead to her sad feelings, physical problems, or problems with her thinking. She did note that she came in to see the psychiatrist only because she didn't "know what else to do."

What's the difference between feeling sad and having depression?

Depression as a medical condition is designated in a category of disorders called depressive disorders. Depressive disorders describe an emotional state of sadness, emptiness, irritability, or difficulty enjoying things that occurs along with physical symptoms or problems with thinking as well as difficulty in daily functioning.[1] More simply put, the diagnosis of a depressive disorder applies when a person has

- a depressed mood or
- trouble enjoying things

accompanied by some or all of the following symptoms:

- changes in sleep (too much or too little)
- changes in appetite (too much or too little)
- decreased energy
- decreased concentration or inability to make decisions
- slow movements or feeling fidgety
- guilty or worthless feelings
- hopeless or suicidal thinking

and

- the person has difficulty functioning in his or her life.

Are there different types of depressive disorders?

Depressive disorders are classified according to the length of time that a person has symptoms, the timing of symptoms, or the cause of symptoms. This chapter focuses mainly on major depressive disorder, or MDD, during which a person experiences (1) a depressed mood or has trouble enjoying things, (2) associated symptoms occurring nearly every day, for most of the day, at least two weeks at a time, and (3) problems functioning at work or with family and friends.[2]

There are special types of major depressive disorders depending on the primary symptoms that a person experiences. *Melancholic depression* occurs when the most notable symptom is a lack of pleasure in activities, and nothing seems to make a person happy. *Atypical depression* is depression that occurs when a person's mood is highly reactive to daily stress, and he or she experiences increased appetite, weight gain, and oversleeping. *Catatonic depression* is when a person becomes extremely depressed and is not able to move his or her body. This type of depression frequently requires hospitalization because the person is not eating or is not able to take care of personal hygiene. It can become a medical emergency because the person is not moving, which puts severe stress on the muscles, leading to muscle deterioration.[3]

Some people experience variation in the timing of their symptoms. *Seasonal pattern depression* is a type of depression in which a person will have depressive symptoms that repeatedly occur or worsen during the winter months and then typically resolve in the spring. When depression occurs in a woman after pregnancy, it is frequently called *postpartum depression*.[4]

It is important for health-care providers to ask details about a person's symptoms and when symptoms occur in order to best understand the type of depression and to provide the most appropriate treatments.

What causes depression, and how is it diagnosed?
Depression is a medical disorder that is related to multiple factors. Variations in brain chemicals, known as neurotransmitters, contribute to the development of depression. Serotonin is the main neurotransmitter that is altered in depression. Family genetics may play a role in development of depression, especially if depression or other psychiatric illnesses run in a person's family. Depression may also occur when a person experiences stress, such as losing a job, relationship problems, or loss of a loved one. Exposure to poverty, neglect, abuse, violence, or other traumas also increase risk for depression. In other cases, depression can occur spontaneously without being related to any particular event.[5]

Unlike such medical conditions as high blood pressure, which is diagnosed by using a blood pressure cuff, or diabetes, which is diagnosed with examination of blood samples, no medical devices or laboratory tests are available to measure neurotransmitter levels to diagnose depression. In order to diagnose depression, a psychiatrist or other health-care provider must interview the patient to ask about depression symptoms.

Psychiatrists or other health-care providers may order blood tests or brain scans to make sure there are no other health conditions that could lead to depression. Thyroid problems, cardiac illness, vitamin deficiencies, diabetes, and cancer are common medical conditions associated with depression.

Psychiatrists or other health-care providers may also ask whether a person is taking medications for other medical problems. Certain types of medications, whether they are prescribed or purchased over the counter, may lead to development of depression.

Depression can also occur if a person uses alcohol and drugs, such as marijuana, cocaine/crack, and opiates (for instance, narcotic pain medications and heroin).[6] Health-care providers must assess for use of alcohol or drugs to determine other potential depression causes.

Who is affected by depression?

Mental health problems, depression in particular, are the leading cause of disability in the United States, more than heart disease or cancer.[7] Looking at the general population, approximately one in six adults will experience depression over the course of their lifetime. At any given time, approximately one in twenty adults will have symptoms consistent with depression. On average, depression symptoms start during the late teenage years through the mid-twenties, although individuals may develop depression during any stage of life. Some experience mild to moderate depression, while others have very severe symptoms where they are not able to function at all.[8]

Overall, women are more likely than men to experience depression. Furthermore, during a woman's lifetime, she is at risk for developing depression for different reasons. For example, between 3 and 6 percent of women develop depression during pregnancy or within weeks and months following delivery. Although the term *postpartum depression* is most commonly used in the media, 50 percent of cases of *post*partum depression actually start *during* pregnancy.[9]

If a woman reports that symptoms occur only before her menstrual period, premenstrual dysphoric disorder (PMDD) may be another depressive disorder to consider. This disorder was previously called premenstrual stress disorder (PMS). Women with this disorder experience mood swings, irritability, interpersonal conflicts, critical thoughts about themselves, and tense feelings. In addition to common physical symptoms and problems with thinking, women with premenstrual dysphoric disorder may also experience breast tenderness or swelling, bloating, and joint or muscle pain.[10]

I heard that black people don't really get depressed. Is that true?

Anyone can be affected by depression. However, studies have shown that depression rates vary among ethnic groups in the United States. Depression rates among black Americans are lower than rates for whites. However, when black Americans experience depression, they are more likely to have longer and more severe courses of depression but are less likely to receive any treatment for their symptoms.[11, 12]

There are a variety of factors contributing to lower rates of depression and depression treatments among black Americans. Depression tends to be diagnosed less often in this population, which may be due to multiple factors, including lack of recognition by providers who may not understand how culture can affect ways that depression is described. Some patients may not say the word *depression* but may describe a depressed mood in other ways: "I feel stressed," "I have the blues," or "I'm feeling some kind of way." In other instances, providers may not recognize signs of depression: "Well, they don't look depressed." Many black Americans put on a mask in order to cope with experiences of racism, sexism, and classism.[13, 14] When a black woman tries to hide her feelings as a coping mechanism, others may see her as a "strong black woman." If a black man tries to hide his feelings as a coping mechanism, others may view him as an "angry black man." These coping mechanisms are used by some black women and men to prevent others from taking advantage of them. Some use these coping mechanisms to protect themselves from feeling too much emotional pain. It is important for health-care providers to have an awareness of stereotypes and an understanding of how their patients may express themselves when they are feeling depressed.

Reliance on informal or nonmedical resources, such as extended family, social networks, and religious/spiritual groups, to help manage depression is also common among black Americans. Some individuals may not want to go to a health-care provider to talk about depression and therefore will not receive a depression diagnosis. In addition, some black Americans are less likely to use formal health-care services. The health-care system is sometimes thought to be untrustworthy due to cases such as the Tuskegee Syphilis Study, in which much-needed treatments were withheld from black patients by the US Public Health Service.[15, 16] Negative beliefs about psychiatric medications can be related to concerns that these medications are used to control patients due to systemic racism within the health-care system.[17, 18] Fear of stigma, worries about addiction or negative side effects of medications, and doubts about whether depression treatments will be helpful are also common causes that may prevent some patients from seeking treatment.[19, 20, 21] To give the best care, it is important for health-care professionals to be aware of how cultural factors affect ways that patients experience depression and seek treatment.

Black people don't commit suicide, do they?

Both patients and health-care providers have debated the myth that black people don't commit suicide.[22] In reality, suicide patterns among black Americans have changed over the past several decades. Black children have experienced a rising suicide rate, while rates among white children have dropped.[23] Across the life span, older white adults commit suicide at the highest rates in the population, but older blacks have the second-highest rate among older adults overall.[24] Suicide methods may also vary by ethnic or racial groups. "Suicide by cop" is a phrase that was created in the 1980s to describe patterns of mostly young black males who instigate conflicts with law enforcement in order to lead officers into shooting them.[25] Some blacks may use other self-destructive ways to attempt or commit suicide, such as not caring for physical health problems or using alcohol or drugs. In essence, both depression and suicide are medical conditions that do in fact affect the black community. Barriers that limit black Americans from seeking treatment must be addressed.

The psychiatrist asked Vivian how she tried to cope with her depression. She reported that she went to church every Sunday and once asked about pastoral counseling. Her pastor offered a chance to come back for counseling, but she never followed up. She confided in her grandmother that she felt sad, but she had not told any family members that she was seeking mental health treatment. She was afraid to come for her appointment because she felt weak that she couldn't control her emotions and make herself feel better. She felt upset after her primary care doctor said that she might need therapy. Vivian said that her primary care doctor prescribed an antidepressant medication, but it did not help.

Can someone make depression go away?

Depression can be treated or managed in several ways. Evidence has shown that black Americans are more likely than whites to have beliefs that depression can be managed by personal will ("pulling yourself up by your bootstraps") or religious/spiritual prayer.[26] Indeed, there are personal approaches that individuals can use to help try to relieve their symptoms, especially when depression is mild. Participating in activities that are pleasurable or rewarding, such as going to social, family, neighborhood, and religious/spiritual functions, can be helpful in alleviating a depressed mood. Exercising may help to improve one's energy but has also been shown to directly improve mood.[27] Other healthy strategies that can help manage symptoms of depression include yoga and meditation.[28] Individuals with depression may find it hard to participate in activities because their motivation may be low. If they wait until they feel better to do things, they might wait a long time and needlessly suffer. Instead, individuals with depression tend to feel better when they start doing things.

Medical treatments for depression can fall into two main categories: talk therapy and medications.

What is talk therapy, and how can it help depression?

Therapy is a way to talk about feelings with the guidance of a professional so that one can feel better and make life changes. Therapy can refer to individual or one-on-one therapy, most often with a psychiatrist, psychologist, or social worker. Therapy can also include group therapy, in which patients with similar problems meet together to evaluate their experiences with the assistance of a therapist. Family or couples therapy can help enhance coping skills for relationship problems. Music and art therapy are options to explore feelings. Because feelings and thoughts are shared in therapy that may have usually been kept private, it can take time to build trust with a provider. For some black patients, it may be particularly important for their therapist to have an awareness of cultural factors that affect their depression.[29]

How do I know if I need therapy or medications?

Depression is a medical condition that can be compared to other illnesses, such as high blood pressure or diabetes. For example, there are approaches that one can use to manage or prevent high blood pressure or diabetes, such as making diet changes, exercising, and maintaining a healthy weight. However, there are times when medications are still needed to help manage these conditions. Because many depressive symptoms are behaviors, some people believe they can just will away depression. However, it is not a common expectation to will blood pressure or blood sugars to be at a particular level, and the same is not possible for depression. In reality, there are things that each person can do, such as the personal approaches previously described, but there are also times when medications are still needed.

Antidepressants are the first category of medications to consider for depression treatment. More specifically, selective serotonin reuptake inhibitors (SSRIs) increase the availability of serotonin in the brain. These medications can help improve mood as well as target associated symptoms, including changes in sleep, appetite, energy, thinking, movements, guilty or worthless feelings, or hopeless feelings.[30]

Potential side effects of antidepressants can include headaches or foggy headedness as the brain adjusts to the medication. This is often a temporary side effect, but if it persists, then the particular antidepressant may not be a good match. Other potential side effects can include nausea, vomiting, or diarrhea as the body adjusts to the medication. Some people also experience weight gain or difficulty losing weight, and some medications are more likely than others to have this side effect. Lastly, for some people, antidepressants can affect interest in sex or the ability to enjoy sex.[31] Sexual side effects are the top reason patients may stop antidepressants, so it is important that health-care professionals provide open discussions about this potentially sensitive topic. Consequently, it is also important to let your provider know if you have any side effects from your medications.

Generally speaking, antidepressants are used to help relieve symptoms of depression, which can help each person to do things that are important in his or her life. If an antidepressant causes intolerable side effects or does not feel helpful, providers can talk about other medications that may be a better match. Nonmental health professionals in such fields as primary care or obstetrics/gynecology can treat patients with mild depression. However, psychiatrists and other mental health-care providers have received specialized training to provide treatments for moderate and severe depression.

If therapy and medications are not helpful or not preferred, other treatments are available that affect brain neurotransmitters to help alleviate depression. Transmagnetic stimulation (TMS), electroconvulsive therapy (ECT), and vagal nerve stimulation (VNS) are examples of nonmedication depression treatments. These procedures are typically provided for patients who do not respond to other depression treatments.[32]

After a few visits with her psychiatrist, who provided therapy along with antidepressant recommendations, Vivian began to talk about concerns that she would become addicted to medications. Her psychiatrist spent time during each visit to explain the potential benefits as well as the risks of antidepressants, noting that antidepressants are not addictive. Vivian then agreed to begin a new antidepressant medication. She talked with her psychiatrist about side effects so that her dose could be slowly increased. As her symptoms began to resolve, Vivian expressed appreciation that she was able to get help for her depression. She developed a new confidence in how to take care of herself to help manage her depression in addition to taking her antidepressant. She was able to perform better at work and enjoyed socializing with friends again.

Who should you call if you think you have depression?

Depression is a medical condition that is common but treatable. Individuals who think they have depression can talk to psychiatrists or other health-care providers for help. It may also be helpful to reach out to trusted family members, friends, or religious figures for support. Support groups provide information online or in person through such organizations as the Depression and Bipolar Support Alliance (DBSA)[33] and the National Alliance on Mental Illness (NAMI).[34]

Notes

1. American Psychiatric Association, "Depressive Disorders," in *Desk Reference to the Diagnostic Criteria from DSM-5* (Washington, DC: American Psychiatric Association, 2013).
2. Ibid.
3. Ibid.
4. Ibid.
5. "What Is Depression?" Ranna Parekh, American Psychiatric Association, accessed December 12, 2017, https://www.psychiatry.org/patients-families/depression/what-is-depression.

6. American Psychiatric Association, "Depressive Disorders."
7. Harvey A. Whiteford, Louisa Degenhardt, Jürgen Rehm, Amanda J. Baxter, Alize J. Ferrari, Holly E. Erskine, Fiona J. Charlson, et al., "Global Burden of Disease Attributable to Mental and Substance Use Disorders: Findings from the Global Burden of Disease Study 2010," *The Lancet* 382, no. 9904 (2013): 1575–86.
8. Ronald C. Kessler, Patricia Berglund, Olga Demler, Robert Jin, Kathleen R. Merikangas, and Ellen E. Walters, "Lifetime Prevalence and Age of Onset Distributions of *DSM-IV* Disorders in the National Comorbidity Survey Replication," *Archives of General Psychiatry* 62, no. 6 (2005): 593–602.
9. American Psychiatric Association, "Depressive Disorders."
10. Ibid.
11. David R. Williams, Hector M. Gonzalez, Harold Neighbors, Randolph Nesse, Jamie M. Abelson, Julie Sweetman, and James S. Jackson, "Prevalence and Distribution of Major Depressive Disorder in African Americans, Caribbean Blacks, and Non-Hispanic Whites: Results from the National Survey of American Life," *Archives of General Psychiatry* 64, no. 3 (2007): 305–15.
12. Harold W. Neighbors, Cleopatra Caldwell, David R. Williams, Randolph Nesse, Robert Joseph Taylor, Kai McKeever Bullard, Myriam Torres, and James S. Jackson, "Race, Ethnicity, and the Use of Services for Mental Disorders: Results from the National Survey of American Life," *Archives of General Psychiatry* 64, no. 4 (2007): 485–94.
13. Lindsey M. West, Roxanne A. Donovan, and Amanda R. Daniel, "The Price of Strength: Black College Women's Perspectives on the Strong Black Woman Stereotype," *Women & Therapy* 39, nos. 3–4 (2016): 390–412.
14. Adia Harvey Wingfield, "The Modern Mammy and the Angry Black Man: African American Professionals' Experiences with Gendered Racism in the Workplace," *Race, Gender & Class* 14, nos. 1/2 (2007): 196–212.
15. Vanessa Northington Gamble, "Under the Shadow of Tuskegee: African Americans and Health Care," *American Journal of Public Health* 87, no. 11 (1997): 1773–78.

16. Matthew K. Wynia and Vanessa Northington Gamble, "Mistrust among Minorities and the Trustworthiness Medicine," *PLoS Medicine* 3, no. 5 (2006): e244.

17. Vicki S. Freimuth, Sandra Crouse Quinn, Stephen B. Thomas, Galen Cole, Eric Zook, and Ted Duncan, "African American's Views on Research and the Tuskegee Syphilis Study," *Social Science & Medicine* 52, no. 5 (2001): 797–808.

18. Alicia K. Matthews, Patrick Corrigan, Barbara M. Smith, and Frances Aranda, "A Qualitative Exploration of African-Americans' Attitudes toward Mental Illness and Mental Illness Treatment Seeking," *Journal of the National Council on Rehabilitation Education* 20, no. 4 (2006): 253–68.

19. Jane L. Givens, Ira R. Katz, Scarlett Bellamy, and William C. Holmes, "Stigma and the Acceptability of Depression Treatments among African Americans and Whites," *Journal of General Internal Medicine* 22, no. 9 (2007): 1292–97.

20. Jason Schnittker, "Misgivings of Medicine? African Americans' Skepticism of Psychiatric Medication," *Journal of Health and Social Behavior* 44, no. 4 (2003): 506–24.

21. Trevor J. Schraufnagel, Amy W. Wagner, Jeanne Miranda, and Peter P. Roy-Byrne, "Treating Minority Patients with Depression and Anxiety: What Does the Evidence Tell Us?" *General Hospital Psychiatry* 28, no. 4 (2006): 517–27.

22. Alvin F. Poussaint and Amy Alexander, *Lay My Burden Down: Suicide and the Mental Health Crisis among African Americans* (Boston, MA: Beacon Press, 2000).

23. "Suicide Rates among Young Black Boys on the Rise," Carina Storrs, CNN, May 19, 2015, http://www.cnn.com/2015/05/19/health/suicide-youth/index.html.

24. Sean Joe, Briggett C. Ford, Robert Joseph Taylor, and Linda M. Chatters, "Prevalence of Suicide Ideation and Attempts among Black Americans in Later Life," *Transcultural Psychiatry* 51, no. 2 (2014): 190–208.

25. Poussaint and Alexander, *Lay My Burden Down*.

26. Leslie C. Jackson and Beverly Greene, eds., *Psychotherapy with African American Women: Innovations in Psychodynamic Perspectives and Practice* (New York: The Guilford Press, 2000).

27. "Depression," National Alliance on Mental Illness, accessed February 19, 2018,http://www.nami.org/Learn-More/Mental-Health-Conditions/Depression/Overview.

28. "Yoga for anxiety and depression," Harvard Medical School, Harvard Health Publishing, accessed February 19, 2018, https://www.health.harvard.edu/mind-and-mood/yoga-for-anxiety-and-depression.

29. Jackson and Greene, *Psychotherapy with African American Women*.

30. "Depression: How effective are antidepressants?" IQWiG (Institute for Quality and Efficiency in Health Care), accessed February 19, 2018, https://www.ncbi.nlm.nih.gov/pubmedhealth/PMH0087089/.

31. Ibid.

32. Ibid.

33. "About the Depression and Bipolar Support Alliance," Depression and Bipolar Support Alliance, accessed December 12, 2017, http://www.dbsalliance.org/site/PageServer?pagename=dbsa_about_dbsa.

34. "About NAMI," National Alliance on Mental Illness, accessed December 12, 2017, https://www.nami.org/About-NAMI.

CHAPTER 3

Bipolar Disorder

Why Do People Keep Telling Me I'm Bipolar?
NAPOLEON B. HIGGINS JR., MD
JAMES LEE JR., MD

"I told my doctor I had mood swings; he told me I have bipolar disorder."

ipolar disorder is one of the most challenging and difficult disorders that psychiatrists treat daily. In this chapter we will discuss what it means to have bipolar disorder. We will talk about the different ways to treat the disorder as well as answer questions about how the disease is diagnosed.

Trinity is a thirty-eight-year-old black female who came in for an evaluation at the partial hospitalization program after being referred by her job. She presented with complaints of episodes of severe depression, stating, "Something is wrong. No matter what I do, my mind won't stop racing, and I can't sleep." She stated that she couldn't go any further and wanted to give up on life. Her job as a midlevel executive is extremely stressful with deadlines, but over the past few weeks she started volunteering to take on multiple projects at work. She was also commended for her extreme work ethic but noticeably was becoming increasingly busy, friendly, chatty, and talkative when she had previously been more reserved. *She returned to work elated and bragging about how she was able to complete a business-related three-week online training course over an extended three-day weekend holiday. Her supervisor said, "There is no way you could have completed that class in three days. You must have gamed the system." Trinity immediately became irate at the accusation and screamed in a staff meeting, "What? You think I had to cheat to get this done because a black woman can't be successful? I've been busting my [expletive] all weekend, been up twenty-four hours straight for four days without a drop of sleep to make sure this project was ready for you ungrateful idiots, and this is all the thanks I get." She continued, and as she became angrier, she began yelling to the point that her speech was incoherent. When she was asked to leave, she started shouting expletives, accused her immediate supervisor of playing favorites due to having an extramarital affair with her coworker, grabbed her purse, and stormed out.*

What is bipolar disorder?

Bipolar disorder is a brain disorder that causes unusual shifts in mood, energy, activity levels, and the ability to carry out everyday tasks. The shifts in mood can range from being very sad and down (depressive episodes) to feeling very hyper, busy, extreme mood swings, or being full of energy (manic episodes).[1]

What is a manic episode?

A manic episode is a period of at least one week of increased, elevated mood. Sometimes people describe themselves as feeling hyper, wired, and overly happy or on top of the world. They may do things that are out of character, such as cleaning when it is not needed, engaging in such pleasure-seeking behavior as risky sexual decisions, or randomly spending excessive amounts of money. There are also periods of being very talkative, speaking so fast that others can't understand what they are saying. They often have rapid thoughts and may go days with requiring very little sleep to not sleeping at all. During these periods, it can be difficult to concentrate and stay on task with daily activities, causing a person to not be able to work or take care of family and individual responsibilities. Many times, manic behavior may require hospitalization due to safety concerns. Sadly, manic behavior often results in incarceration due to poor decision-making being mistaken as deliberate criminal activity. This is especially true for African Americans.[2]

In some cases, the individual may have hypomanic episodes that are like manic behavior but are not as severe. Often when individuals have hypomanic episodes, they are not as noticeable and may find that they are more productive than normal. If a person has hypomanic episodes but has never had a full manic episode, then the person will be diagnosed with bipolar II disorder, described further later in this chapter.

What is a depressive episode?

A depressive episode is a period of at least two weeks when you may feel sad or down, have decreased energy or motivation, and have changes in how you sleep or in your appetite. The decreased energy or motivation may be to a level that you don't get out of bed or go to work. There may be periods of guilt, a decreased interest in things you enjoy, or even thoughts of worthlessness and feeling like life is not worth living. The combination of depression with hopeless and helpless feelings can lead to suicidal thinking.

It is not uncommon for a person to have both manic and depressive symptoms at the same time, having a *mixed* presentation. Some others will go back and forth between depression and mania over several days or even daily. This is often referred to as rapid cycling or ultra-rapid cycling. In severe cases a person may hear voices or develop delusions and have psychotic features.

What are the symptoms of bipolar disorder?

People who are diagnosed with bipolar disorder can have periods of feeling *depressed* or sad for long periods of time as well as having unexplained crying, decreased interest in activities, and a lack of energy. There may be problems with sleeping, eating, and thoughts of death. In addition, there can also be periods of *mania*, such as feeling restless and having too much energy. People may feel very irritable or quick to anger, argue a lot, have to have the last word, start "going off" or "poppin' off," and feel full of themselves. They can have periods of poor judgment, distraction, rapid speech, and thoughts that won't shut off. During these episodes, patients might not need much sleep and feel impulsive. They can also exhibit dangerous or reckless behavior, such as spending money they don't have or having an increased number of sexual encounters.

Is bipolar disorder the same as being manic depressive?

Manic-depressive disorder and bipolar disorder are usually used to describe the same thing. Psychiatrists, psychologists, and other people who work in mental health use the term *bipolar disorder*. Many people who have the disorder use the term *manic depressive* because it describes the two parts of the disease: depression and mania.[3]

Can I have a depressive or manic episode without the other and still be diagnosed with bipolar disorder?

A person diagnosed with bipolar I disorder or bipolar II disorder must have at least one manic/hypomanic episode during his or her lifetime. If he or she has not had mania or hypomania, there may be another disorder that needs to be considered and correctly diagnosed. Many people describe mania as a good feeling or feeling they are "high," and most will not notice feeling high as a problem. A person with bipolar disorder may not have the insight to recognize the symptoms of mania. Instead, others around him or her are more likely to notice mania because of the change in behavior. Depression is more easily recognized by those who are experiencing it. Therefore, individuals with bipolar disorder tend to bring themselves in for treatment during depressive episodes because they "*feel* depressed." However, when mania occurs, they are often brought into treatment due to their "*acting* manic."

How is bipolar disorder diagnosed?

Bipolar disorder is diagnosed by having an evaluation with a psychiatrist or mental health professional. The mental health provider will complete an assessment after he or she conducts the initial evaluation. There are not currently any blood tests or brain scans that can diagnose bipolar disorder. Therefore, it is important to be open and honest with your doctor when discussing your symptoms because the information gathered during the evaluation is used in making a correct diagnosis.

What is the difference between bipolar I disorder, bipolar II disorder, and bipolar mixed episodes?

The main difference between bipolar I and bipolar II disorders is whether there is a manic episode or a hypomanic episode. A manic episode usually lasts up to a week or longer and causes some impairment or limitations at home, school, or work. If a person has a manic episode and a history of a depressive episode, he or she can be diagnosed with bipolar I disorder. A hypomanic episode usually lasts at least four days in a row. The symptoms of a hypomanic episode are usually not as severe as with a manic episode. If a person has a hypomanic episode and a history of experiencing a depressive episode, he or she can be diagnosed with bipolar II disorder. Patients may also be diagnosed as having bipolar mixed episodes when they are experiencing both manic and depressive symptoms at the same time.[4]

Trinity later stated that during and immediately after college, "Everything just seemed to go right." She was married for five years, but the arguing wouldn't stop. The marriage continued worsening, and her husband left after she spent the deposit they had been saving for a home on a "weekend car." She tried multiple medications on and off for many years but felt they either didn't work or made her feel worse, and one made her turn into a "chatterbox" because her mind wouldn't stop racing.

Can bipolar disorder be diagnosed in children?

Bipolar disorder can be difficult to diagnose in children due to manic-like symptoms being confused with other factors of a child's behavior.[5] It is very important that a psychiatrist or mental health provider make this diagnosis. A child or adolescent may not have the same symptoms as an adult when diagnosed with bipolar disorder. This is discussed further in chapter 8.

When discussing her childhood, Trinity further described that these symptoms began when she was in middle school, where she blamed her behavior on being a "hormonal, mood-swinging, and rebellious teenager." She once got into a shouting match with her mother during a meeting with the school principal. She ended up hitting a school officer who attempted to intervene during the meeting. She spent two weeks in a psychiatric hospital. She stated that she made a lot of poor sexual decisions in high school and just could not say no to guys.

What medications are used to treat bipolar disorder?

There are several different types of medications that are used to treat bipolar disorder. These medications are usually classified as mood stabilizers, atypical antipsychotics, and/or antidepressants. It will be up to the psychiatrist to decide which medications are used based on the individual's needs.[6] These medications are further discussed in chapter 10.

Do I need to be treated for bipolar disorder if I'm not showing any symptoms?

Once the diagnosis of bipolar disorder is made, medications and talk therapy (psychotherapy) are usually suggested. Even if you are not showing symptoms, it is important to start and continue medications once the diagnosis is made. Continuing medications despite not having symptoms may prevent the symptoms from returning. It may also decrease how severe the symptoms are if they return. Bipolar disorder is a chronic condition. There is no cure;

however, being on the right combination of medications, diet, and lifestyle can help to decrease the severity of the mood swings and other symptoms.[7, 8]

After careful consideration of Trinity's current state and past symptoms, she was diagnosed with bipolar I disorder and admitted into the partial hospitalization program, where she received daily group and individual therapy over the course of three weeks. She was started on a mood stabilizer, and she noticed improvement in her depression and mood swings in about a week or so. She increased her church attendance and began going to women's groups for increased positive social interactions. She changed her diet and wanted to take an approach to her mental health that included medications, exercise, nutrition, and individual talk therapy. After a month, she was cleared to return to work on a part-time basis for approximately two weeks before returning to her regular work schedule. She learned to achieve balance and educate herself on her illness and how to better recognize symptoms. She learned to not overwhelm herself and stated she would continue to work on "being the best me that I can be."

In summary, bipolar disorder is a very challenging disorder to diagnose and treat. It takes a careful and thoughtful approach from the psychiatrist and a patient who is truthful and honest with his or her doctor. Bipolar disorder is caused by a chemical imbalance that does require treatment with medications. In addition, counseling can also help with coping with stressors and difficult situations. Once diagnosed and treated correctly, it is possible to have a productive life and to return to a baseline level of functioning.[9, 10]

Notes

1. American Psychiatric Association, *Diagnostic and Statistical Manual of Mental Disorders*, 5th ed. (Washington, DC: American Psychiatric Association, 2013), 124–25.
2. Mark Bauer, Jürgen Unützer, Harold A. Pincus, and William B. Lawson, "Bipolar Disorder," *Mental Health Services Research* 4, no. 4 (2002): 225–29.

3. Robert Hirschfeld and Lana A. Vornik, "Perceptions and Impact of Bipolar Disorder: How Far Have We Really Come? Results of the National Depressive and Manic-Depressive Association 2000 Survey of Individuals with Bipolar Disorder," *The Journal of Clinical Psychiatry* 64, no. 2 (2003): 402–07.

4. Rakesh Jain, Vladimir Maletic, and Roger S. McIntyre, "Diagnosing and Treating Patients with Mixed Features," *The Journal of Clinical Psychiatry* 78, no. 8 (2017): 1091–1102.

5. Carl C. Bell and Radhika Chimata, "Prevalence of Neurodevelopmental Disorders among Low-Income African Americans at a Clinic on Chicago's South Side," *Psychiatric Services* 66, no. 5 (2015): 539–42.

6. David C. Henderson, "Weight Gain with Atypical Antipsychotics: Evidence and Insights," *The Journal of Clinical Psychiatry* 68, suppl. 12 (2006): 18–26.

7. Francesco Colom, Eduard Vieta, Anabel Martínez-Arán, María Reinares, José Manuel Goikolea, Antonio Benabarre, Carla Torrent, et al., "A Randomized Trial on the Efficacy of Group Psychoeducation in the Prophylaxis of Recurrences in Bipolar Patients Whose Disease Is in Remission," *Archives of General Psychiatry* 60, no. 4 (2003): 402–07.

8. Louisa G. Sylvia, Stephanie Salcedo, Emily E. Bernstein, Ji Hyun Baek, Andrew A. Nierenberg, and Thilo Deckersbach, "Nutrition, Exercise, and Wellness Treatment in Bipolar Disorder: Proof of Concept for a Consolidated Intervention," *International Journal of Bipolar Disorders* 1, no. 1 (2013): 1–24.

9. David Lachar, Sonja L. Randle, Andrew Harper, Kathy C. Scott-Gurnell, Kay R. Lewis, Cynthia W. Santos, Ann E. Saunders, Deborah A. Pearson, Katherine A. Loveland, and Sharon T. Morgan, "The Brief Psychiatric Rating Scale for Children (BPRS-C): Validity and Reliability of an Anchored Version," *Journal of the American Academy of Child & Adolescent Psychiatry* 40, no. 3 (2001): 333–40.

10. Karen Dineen Wagner, Robert M. A. Hirschfeld, Graham Emslie, Robert Findling, Barbara L. Gracious, and Michael L. Reed, "Validation of the Mood Disorder Questionnaire for Bipolar Disorders in Adolescents," *The Journal of Clinical Psychiatry* 67, no. 5 (2006): 827–30.

CHAPTER 4

Anxiety Disorders

Is This Just Nerves?
JAMES LEE JR., MD

"I'm not crazy; I just need something for my nerves."

Psychiatrists and other mental health providers hear the preceding comments daily. In this chapter we will explain what anxiety is and why it causes so many problems in our lives. We will address the different kinds of anxiety and how mental health providers treat these issues. Overall, people more often present with problems caused by anxiety compared to any other mental health disorders.[1] Anxiety is the most common reason that people seek help. Many people describe it as having nerve problems or being a worry wart. In the African American community, anxiety disorders are 20 percent less prevalent than in Caucasian communities.[2] In addition, women have been found to be more likely than men to be diagnosed with an anxiety disorder. There is no single reason for these differences. Knowing and understanding when an individual needs help and a person's ability to cope and deal with stress all play a part in the reasoning.

What causes anxiety?

Anxiety doesn't necessarily have to be caused by anything. Anxiety is often a normal reaction to stress. In some cases it can be useful because it can help alert a person to strange or dangerous situations. However, an anxiety disorder is not helpful and usually causes some problems in your life and can affect work or school.

What are the different types of anxiety disorders?

Anxiety disorders include panic disorder, agoraphobia, specific phobia, and social anxiety disorder. One other diagnosis, posttraumatic stress disorder (PTSD), is also very common; however, it will be discussed in chapter 5.

How are anxiety disorders diagnosed?

A detailed interview is needed to diagnose an anxiety disorder. During the interview, the provider will ask questions to better understand the problems that the individual is currently having. It is possible to have symptoms of more than one anxiety disorder at the same time.

What is generalized anxiety disorder?

Generalized anxiety disorder (GAD) is excessive anxiety and worry occurring a majority of the time for at least six months. Physically, there can be symptoms of fatigue, irritability, restlessness, difficulty in concentrating, muscle tension, and problems with sleep.[3] It is totally appropriate to worry about specific things from time to time. For example, if there are legitimate problems that are causing stressors, it is OK to have some level of anxiety. However, individuals with generalized anxiety disorder usually worry far more about trivial, everyday occurrences. In addition, the episodes usually affect them socially or in a work setting. Individuals often complain of having racing thoughts, not being able to focus, or "being a worry wart." Generalized anxiety disorder is one of the most common anxiety disorders. There have not been any studies to highlight any differences in the African American community.[4]

What is obsessive compulsive disorder?

Obsessive compulsive disorder (OCD) is a condition highlighted by obsessions (recurrent, intrusive thoughts) that are relieved by physical actions known as compulsions. Obsessions are unwanted or intrusive thoughts or urges that continuously occur. Meanwhile, compulsions are repetitive behaviors that help to decrease stress associated with the obsessive thought.[5] The behaviors can be identified as checking and rechecking items, hand washing, and so on, whereas the mental acts can be such activities as praying, counting, or repeating words or phrases. These individuals usually realize that their actions or thoughts are not "normal." The repetitiveness of the thoughts or behavior often causes problems in some level of daily function. However, some do not realize that their issues are a treatable psychiatric illness.

What is panic disorder?

Panic disorder is a condition in which you worry excessively about having repeated panic attacks. Individuals sometime worry to the point that they isolate themselves and do not enjoy going out in public. Sometimes people with panic disorder can go out in public but only in familiar places.

Is there a difference between a panic attack and an anxiety attack?

Panic attacks and anxiety attacks are the same thing. A panic attack is a sudden, unexpected sense of fear or discomfort that is accompanied by certain physical symptoms. These symptoms range from sweating, racing heart, fearing losing control or dying, shaking or tremors, feeling lightheaded or dizzy, having shortness of breath, feeling detached from oneself, experiencing chest pain, nausea, numbness, or tingling within the extremities or face, and having chills or feeling as if one is choking. Some individuals complain of feeling like they "are going crazy" or having a heart attack.

If I have a panic attack, do I have panic disorder?

Panic disorder is diagnosed only when you have repeated panic attacks and begin to fear or anticipate having another one. This anticipation leads to excessive worrying and finding ways to avoid certain stressors that are thought to contribute to the panic attacks. *Agoraphobia* is another term that is used when discussing panic disorder. It is the fear of being in open or enclosed spaces, being in unfamiliar places alone, or being in crowds. In addition, the fear of being in this situation is exaggerated. People have a fear of not being able to escape from a situation and try to avoid the situation altogether.[6]

What are phobias?

Phobias represent a fear of a specific object or situation. These objects and/or situations include but are not limited to spiders, snakes and insects, water, heights and flying, elevators, escalators, and other enclosed spaces. The object almost always creates an increased level of anxiety. As with other anxiety disorders, the presenting symptoms are usually out of proportion to the situation.

What is social anxiety disorder?

Social anxiety disorder is an increase in anxiety or fear in any social situation, especially if it is a possibility of being judged or observed by others. Individuals can be afraid to perform or talk in front of others, even if they are around people they know. Sometimes there can be problems with common, everyday activities, such as eating and drinking in public. With social anxiety disorder, people are afraid of being judged or embarrassed even when they have not done anything embarrassing. This fear prevents individuals from following through with basic daily tasks.

Regardless of the presentation, most if not all of the individuals seeking treatment have common questions about their disorders. First and foremost, they want to make sure they aren't "crazy." Many of these individuals have been made to think there is not any basis for the symptoms they are currently experiencing when in fact there is often a biological reason behind the actual disorder. The clinician should help them understand that, in some cases, the anxiety disorder is a chronic illness like hypertension, high cholesterol, or diabetes. However, in some cases it has been caused due to some conflict or stressors.

Jason is a thirty-one-year-old male with episodes of dizziness, nausea, ringing in his ears (vertigo), and heart racing (palpitations) after all other medical tests were negative. He had been having problems for over four months. When he had periods of nausea and feeling as if the room were spinning, he would also have feelings of "impending doom." He found himself having racing thoughts, especially at night. He also constantly worried about things he had no control over. His family doctor saw him initially, and after evaluation, referred him to four different specialists. All their tests were negative as well. Jason was becoming frustrated that none of the doctors could find out why he was having these problems.

Finally, Jason was seen by a psychiatrist who was able to discover why he was having these physical symptoms. Jason was diagnosed with generalized anxiety disorder. In his case, he worried excessively and had periods of racing thoughts. These symptoms of anxiety were accompanied by physical symptoms that included feeling dizzy, being irritable, and having a fast, unsteady heart rate (palpitations) and nausea. At his worst, he had a sense of "feeling as if something bad was going to happen." He was started on a small dose of an antidepressant and reevaluated in four to six weeks. However, he did not start the medication immediately. He continued to have exacerbations of anxiety and had another severe panic attack a few days after his appointment. He admitted being in denial about having an anxiety disorder and being frustrated that there wasn't a physical explanation as to why he was having these problems. After having the last panic attack, he was more accepting of taking the medication. He started the prescribed medication and within the next few weeks noticed a significant improvement in his symptoms.

This case represents a few of the ways individuals dealing with anxiety present to their doctors. Some people believe they are losing control or "going crazy." Others believe there must be a physical explanation for how they are feeling. They have a better understanding of their symptoms only after exhausting other resources, doctors' appointments, and/or other tests. Many people find out they have problems with anxiety after going to the emergency room for experiencing chest pain. It is only after the medical tests result in no physical explanations that these individuals are commonly referred to a psychiatrist or mental health professional. Only with the teamwork of both patients and providers can the right approach be taken to help them return to their normal functioning.

A thirty-two-year-old female, Anika, presented with numerous complaints surrounding anxiety. She constantly worried about things she could not control. She was always in fear anytime her children had to leave the house. She would turn a simple situation into a catastrophe. The periods of excessive worrying caused her to keep to herself and to not want to leave the house. She remembers having her first panic attack at the age of twelve. However, her symptoms were getting worse and affecting her quality of life and her ability to care for her children. She would constantly fear getting in an accident while she was driving. She would be afraid that her children would be kidnapped if they were out of her sight. She would also think that common physical problems, such as headaches or stomachaches, were severe medical illnesses, including a brain tumor or cancer.

After her doctor's appointment, she was started on an antidepressant to help treat the symptoms of anxiety. She was scared to take the medication because she thought she would die from the side effects. After the next few appointments, her questions were answered, and she finally decided to take the medication. After starting the medication, she began to notice an improvement. She did not have the racing thoughts as frequently. She did not worry excessively and feel paranoid about being in public. She could complete daily tasks without having thoughts about what "would or could happen." More importantly, she found a job and eventually got her own apartment. She was able to provide more for herself and her children and felt much more positive about herself and her situation.

If I have problems with anxiety, what are my treatment options?

There are several different ways to treat anxiety disorders. The combination of using medications and therapy usually works best in treating problems with anxiety. The class of medications called antidepressants is mainly used to treat anxiety. When involved in therapy, several approaches to counseling, such as cognitive behavioral therapy or exposure and response prevention, are used to alleviate symptoms.

I'm not feeling depressed; why am I being prescribed antidepressants?

The term *antidepressants* is used to describe a group of medications used in psychiatry. Although they do treat depression, this is not the only thing they are used for. They are the preferred group of medications when treating anxiety as well.

What other types of medications are used to treat anxiety?

Benzodiazepines can be used initially or on an as-needed basis to help decrease symptoms of anxiety. However, people can get addicted to these medications if they are not used appropriately. There is also an increased risk of abuse with these medications. Another group of medications, beta blockers, can also be used to help decrease some of the symptoms noted in anxiety disorders, especially tremors and increased pulse and heart rate. Using any medication has its benefits as well as possible side effects and should be done under the supervision of a licensed doctor.

Will I have to take this medication for the rest of my life?

Each case within psychiatry is different. However, for most people, the medication helps to decrease the symptoms and to get them through the day without considerable problems. Without the medication, many of the symptoms that the medication is helping would return. Therefore, the medication would be used on a long-term basis, much like most blood pressure and diabetic medications.

I don't want to take another pill. Is medication the only answer?

In addition to medication management, there are other options that are successful in treating anxiety disorders. Some individuals, when motivated, are solely able to use these techniques to help decrease their symptoms. Studies have suggested that more than 75 percent of people prefer psychotherapy to medication management.[7] One area of treatment is cognitive behavioral therapy (CBT). When using CBT, people learn how to isolate negative thoughts and destructive behaviors. They replace these negative thoughts with more positive ideas and help increase happiness and self-esteem. Although this line of therapy has been very successful in treating social anxiety disorder, it has also been used repeatedly among providers to treat a variety of anxiety disorders. Exposure and response prevention is mainly used in OCD to help decrease compulsive behaviors associated with certain rituals. In doing so, the object is to decrease the resulting anxiety associated with the action. Many associated treatment options are utilized within CBT or exposure and response prevention, such as certain breathing exercises, relaxation techniques, and/or biofeedback to help to alleviate symptoms of anxiety.

In summary, all anxiety disorders are not treated the same. It is often believed that anxiety is caused by physical problems; however, by definition, anxiety is the body's natural response to any conflict. There are some instances for which there are no specific situations that cause symptoms of anxiety. People usually seek some type of assistance when the level of anxiety causes problems in some area of everyday life. Finally, when treating anxiety, some are treated with medications, some are treated with counseling or therapy, and some are treated with both. It takes both the patient and the provider working together to find the right approach to help the patient return to his or her baseline level of functioning.

Notes

1. "Anxiety Disorders," National Alliance on Mental Illness, accessed February 8, 2018, https://www.nami.org/Learn-More/Mental-Health-Conditions/Anxiety-Disorders.

2. "Anxiety Disorders," National Institute of Mental Health, accessed February 8, 2018, https://www.nimh.nih.gov/health/topics/anxiety-disorders/index.shtml.

3. American Psychiatric Association, *Diagnostic and Statistical Manual of Mental Disorders*, 5th ed. (Washington, DC: American Psychiatric Association, 2013), 222.

4. "Anxiety Disorders," National Institute of Mental Health, accessed February 8, 2018, https://www.nimh.nih.gov/health/topics/anxiety-disorders/index.shtml.

5. American Psychiatric Association, *Diagnostic and Statistical Manual of Mental Disorders*, 237–39.

6. Ibid., 208–14.

7. Falk Leichsenring and Christiane Steinert, "Is Cognitive Behavioral Therapy the Gold Standard for Psychotherapy? The Need for Plurality in Treatment and Research," *Journal of the American Medical Association* 318, no. 14 (2017): 1323–24.

CHAPTER 5
PTSD and Trauma

Why Can't I Just Let It Go?

OTIS ANDERSON III, MD

Alex is a twenty-one-year-old male who was referred for treatment by a concerned family member. Alex was referred for treatment secondary to his varied substance abuse. His family had been concerned about his poor motivation and drive, his inability to keep a job, and his explosive moods. Alex said that "nothing is wrong" but admits to having difficulty sleeping and using drugs and alcohol to "help me sleep and calm my nerves."

When Alex was growing up, he lived in a chaotic household. His parents did not get along, and he witnessed violent fights between his mother and father. His mother stabbed his father during one explosive incident; however, his father refused to press charges. His two-year-old half-brother was found dead when Alex was six, and the mother of his half brother was later charged with his death. His parents decided to divorce when he was twelve. At that time his grades started to decline, and his mother sent him to stay with his father. Alex admitted that he started hanging out with a bad crowd at that time. His friends would often smoke marijuana and skip school.

Alex admitted to losing his virginity at the age of thirteen to a seventeen-year-old girl who would babysit him at his father's home. Alex would *later drop out of high school in the eleventh grade. However, he completed his GED. Alex started working after high school but lost his job after six years. He enrolled in junior college and completed coursework to get an associate's degree in business management. He had worked two additional retail jobs but lost both due to failed drug tests.*

When children and adults experience traumatic life events, it can be devastating. This experience can affect their everyday lives as well as their personal growth and development. When most people think of children and trauma, they think that children are resilient and can easily overcome negative events over time. This isn't necessarily true. In fact children respond to trauma much like adults, and in some instances the side effects are more severe. Children tend to hold their negative feelings inside because they have not fully developed their coping skills.

When people are exposed to trauma or multiple traumas, they can develop a disorder known as posttraumatic stress disorder, or PTSD as it is more commonly called. PTSD is a mental illness where the person may have a great deal of emotional distress. The level of distress is sometimes so high that the person can't function in the way he or she may have before the trauma.

What is PTSD?

PTSD is a disorder that is often identified in veterans. However, it is not a disorder that is only experienced by veterans. According to the National Institute of Mental Health, PTSD can be attributed to any chronic feelings of anxiety following exposure to or direct experience of a dangerous event. Dangerous events can include many types of stressful events, such as car accidents, being a victim of a crime, or living in an environment where violence happens regularly. The more we acknowledge and recognize this disorder, the greater the potential to help those who suffer from it.

If PTSD goes untreated, children and adolescents can be negatively affected in multiple areas of their lives.[1] When they receive treatment early after experiencing trauma, those negative symptoms can be drastically reduced. PTSD is a disorder that is characterized by anxiety. This fear or anxiety is generally related to something that happened in the person's life that caused him or her great mental stress. Some of the most common causes are in response to death or loss, being threatened with death, serious injuries to themselves or others, or being violated sexually.[2] With PTSD, the person is usually directly involved in the event, he or she has witnessed the event, such as the death of a loved one, or the person is in an environment where he or she is repeatedly exposed to trauma. Such individuals may also have people around them who reinforce their negative feelings about a previous traumatic event.

How do you know PTSD when you see it?

The following list is a sample of some of the behaviors you may witness in a child or adult who is suffering from PTSD:[3]

- Wetting the bed outside of times when it is age appropriate
- Seeing or hearing things that may not be there (sometimes related to what caused the trauma)
- Being very jumpy or easily scared
- Having trouble sleeping through the night, which may be caused by nightmares or sleepwalking
- Having a fear of interacting with people, visiting places, or being in situations that did not cause fear before the trauma
- Having no interest in things they once cared for
- Exhibiting mood swings
- Having moods that change from one state to another very quickly
- Being more aware of things around them in comparison to before the event
- Having severe crying spells
- Having an increased desire to be alone or an increased need to be with other people at all times
- Feeling fear of things that did not cause fear before the trauma (for example, fear of the dark)

The experience of some of these symptoms may indicate that a person is suffering from posttraumatic stress disorder. It is important to note that the presence of PTSD depends on the individual and the factors related to the trauma.

What behaviors are associated with PTSD in children and adolescents?

When children and adolescents suffer from PTSD, they can have disruptions in many areas, and sometimes all areas, of their lives. They may find it hard to focus, which could cause their grades to fall. They may be nervous, overly alert, on edge, or afraid they are in danger. They may not be interested in being with their friends, and those relationships may suffer because they want to be alone more than they want to socialize. Sometimes they may act out in ways that cause them hurt or harm. If the symptoms are not treated, there is a great chance they will become more severe.

Alex has been having problems sleeping at night. He wakes up in cold sweats, often haunted by the same nightmares—that he will be shot. Alex has been having problems focusing on his job and frequently gets into arguments with peers. He has been fired from multiple jobs for exercising poor attention to detail and having extensive absences from work with little explanation.

How is PTSD treated?

If you feel like you or someone you know may have symptoms of PTSD, it is important to consult with a psychiatrist as soon as possible. The earlier the person is able to begin a course of treatment, the better. Sometimes people will dismiss or ignore the signs and will seek help only when they are unable to function normally.

If the symptoms have increased or more symptoms have been identified, there is a second option of residential treatment. Residential treatment is when people spend time at a treatment center for approximately thirty days. These types of programs have been found to be very useful in helping children and adolescents successfully learn to cope with some of the difficulties related to their illness.

Residential facilities allow them to get away from their daily routines and experiences. In these programs, children are given an opportunity to actively work on their feelings in an environment that is safe, secure, and nonjudgmental. The only role they have is to work on feeling better. In treatment, they are provided with support from trained professionals who can help them work through negative memories and triggers. These professionals work with them to provide coping skills they can use with confidence when they complete the treatment program.

Children and adolescents who enter into a residential program also have the support of others in their age group who may be dealing with some of the same struggles. This is sometimes beneficial because the children don't feel like they are alone in how they may feel. Residential programs may help children and adolescents take a positive first step toward a more fulfilling future.[4]

What if drugs are also involved?

Adults who have PTSD and abuse a substance should seek substance abuse treatment coupled with therapy to uncover the source of why they choose to self-medicate through substance abuse. For those people who may be living in high-risk environments, it is important that they seek help from someone or a program that is sensitive to the influence their environment has on their abuse. Those who have high-risk careers, such as military personnel, law enforcement officers, emergency medical personnel, and firefighters, can also be at an increased risk of substance abuse.

Most recently, there has been additional research on those who are growing up in impoverished or inner-city areas. Sometimes people in these areas are exposed to trauma more often and may live in a constant state of fear and danger. Many become overwhelmed by incidents of domestic violence or sudden loss of loved ones due to crimes because they happen so frequently.

In one study, researchers interviewed more than eight thousand inner-city residents. Approximately 66 percent of respondents said they had been victims of violent attacks at some point in their lives. Fifty percent personally knew a murder victim. Regarding the women in the study, approximately 33 percent had been sexually assaulted. Roughly one in three respondents had experienced symptoms indicative of PTSD. This rate was as high as, and in some cases higher than, that experienced by veterans of the Vietnam, Iraq, and Afghanistan wars.[5]

How can I help a loved one or family member get treatment?

If you know someone who is suffering from PTSD, it can be very hard. You may feel hurt and unable to figure out how to help him or her. If your loved one has experienced a traumatic event and you have noticed some of the behaviors discussed in this chapter, it may be time to seek help from a mental health professional.

Notes

1. Sean Perrin, "Children Exposed to Trauma Should Be Screened for Symptoms of PTSD," *Evidence-Based Mental Health* 17, no. 4 (2014): 107.

2. Leslie C. Rideout and Patricia A. Normandin, "Pediatric Post-Traumatic Stress Disorder," *Journal of Emergency Nursing* 41, no. 6 (2015): 531–32.

3. American Psychiatric Association, *Diagnostic and Statistical Manual of Mental Disorders*, 5th ed. (Washington, DC: American Psychiatric Association, 2013).

4. Shamra Marie Boel-Studt, "A Quasi-Experimental Study of Trauma-Informed Psychiatric Residential Treatment for Children and Adolescents," *Research on Social Work Practice* 27, no. 3 (2017): 273–82.

5. Naomi Breslau, "Trauma and Mental Health in US Inner-City Populations," *General Hospital Psychiatry* 31, no. 6 (2009): 501–02.

CHAPTER 6
Schizophrenia and Psychosis

Why Do Some People Hear Voices?
TEO-CARLO STRAUN, MD

Winston is a twenty-one-year-old African American male with poor grooming and hygiene and a strong smell of tobacco. He showed up at the psychiatric emergency room (ER) with a police officer who claimed that the patient confronted him and adamantly asked him to shoot him. The police officer also reported that the patient claimed he would be able to stop the bullet with his thoughts and asked the cop to bow down and pray to him.

During the interview, the patient was quite paranoid, with poor eye contact, and refused to say much. When asked about his mood, he described it by saying, "I'm OK. Not sure why I am here," yet he appeared very tense at times and gave a blank stare. He talked slowly with a robotic tone. He denied any thoughts of hurting others or himself and mumbled softly to himself. He occasionally looked at the ceiling and shouted, "Someone is playing mind games with me" and "I am tired of hearing these voices in my head." With his hand on his head, he then asked the doctor, "Am I crazy?"

Is Winston going crazy?

What is crazy? *Webster Dictionary* defines it as being "mad, insane, out of the ordinary"; however, it is often used to describe different types of people and scenarios. It is generally accepted that a person with schizophrenia is crazy. But many consider a stalker is crazy. A funny person is crazy. A lady with eight cats is crazy. Your ex is crazy. In the voice of Martin Lawrence, "You so crazy!" We even have scales for crazy. You can be little crazy, good crazy, and certifiably crazy. Crazy can even be urbanized and shortened to "cray cray." With so many common ways to define crazy, it is important to note that *crazy* has a negative stigma, is not a medical term, and may be a reason people often struggle to seek help.

In this chapter we will explore the different types of psychotic disorders, such as schizophrenia, and emphasize the importance of obtaining an accurate diagnosis and treatment.

What is psychosis?

Psychosis is a symptom, not an illness, and is very common, with approximately one hundred thousand young people experiencing psychosis each year. Psychosis refers to a loss of contact with reality or having difficulty determining what is real from what is not real. It is also an umbrella term for a wide variety of disorders. When someone is psychotic, it means that he or she is experiencing one (or more) of the following symptoms:[1]

- **Delusions:** False, rigid, and fixed beliefs about something despite strong contradictory evidence. Delusions can be bizarre or non-bizarre.
- **Bizarre delusions:** The belief is false, clearly implausible, and not derived from ordinary life experiences (for example, aliens implanted a microchip in your brain).[2]
  - **Non-bizarre delusions:** The belief is false but at least within the realm of possibility (for example, believing that you are under constant police surveillance or that people are out to harm you or are plotting against you).

- **Hallucinations:** A perception of something that isn't present. Hallucinations can affect all five senses (hearing, taste, sight, touch, and smell). The most common types of hallucinations are visual (sight) and auditory (hearing).
- **Visual hallucinations:** A person may see things that aren't there (for example, insects crawling on your body or on someone else).
- **Auditory hallucinations:** When one hears voices that aren't there (for example, the voices are talking to each other or telling you to do something).
  - **Disordered thinking:** This symptom makes it very difficult to think straight or communicate. Speech is disordered and may result in poor focus, concentration, distraction, and impaired reasoning. The person may stop conversation midsentence, jump from topic to topic, and say words that do not make sense to the observer. Disordered thinking often leads to social isolation because of issues with communication and is a characteristic feature of schizophrenia.

After the initial ER psychiatric evaluation, Winston was suspected of having a psychotic disorder, but further information would be needed from family and friends to accurately determine the type of disorder from which he suffered.

His mother, who is a political science college professor, told the psychiatrist that she had a normal pregnancy and that Winston had a normal childhood but was often very quiet. She frequently wondered if her arguments with her husband may have had an adverse effect on his mental state. Otherwise, there was no formal history that she knew of but was certain that her husband's family is "all crazy."

What are the different types of psychotic disorders?[3]

Substance-induced psychosis. This includes psychotic symptoms caused by use of or withdrawal from certain addictive substances. The most common ones are alcohol and illicit drugs, such as marijuana, LSD, acid, mushrooms, crystal meth, cocaine, and so on. Substance-induced psychosis will usually go away on its own once the person stops taking drugs. Usually the symptoms go away once the drug wears off, although it is possible for some people to continue to have psychotic symptoms long after the substance has left the body.

Psychosis due to a general medical condition. Sometimes a person has psychotic symptoms because of a general medical condition rather than a mental illness. A brain tumor, stroke, urinary tract infection, or recent surgery can result in confusion, disorientation, and often hallucinations or delusions. A patient can even become psychotic after a prolonged stay in the hospital.

Major depressive disorder with psychotic features. This is also called psychotic depression, which is a serious illness during which a person suffers from the combination of depressed mood and psychosis. It is extremely common in older adults, and the psychotic symptoms in psychotic depression often occur during the depressive episode.

Bipolar disorder in a manic episode. Bipolar disorder is characterized by unusual shifts in mood, alternating between depression and mania. Mania is characterized by a period of a persistently elevated and euphoric mood, decreased need for sleep, rapid speech, increased goal-directed activity (such as staying up all night to plan world domination), and reckless behavior, such as gambling, sexual promiscuity, or spending large sums of money on things that one may not need. When people are manic, they often become psychotic. People who are manic may have mood symptoms consistent with grandiose delusions. They may think they are the president of the United States, Jesus, and so on, often accompanied by auditory hallucinations ("everyone is crazy but me").

Delusional disorder. Delusional disorder is diagnosed when a person is otherwise "normal" but has an unshakable, false belief that he or she continues to believe even in the face of evidence to the contrary. For example, a woman who becomes absolutely fixated on the idea that her husband is cheating on her, with no evidence to support it, may have a delusional disorder.

Primary psychotic disorders. Primary psychotic disorders are long-term psychotic disorders (lasting for a minimum of one month) and include schizophrenia and schizoaffective disorder (which is schizophrenia that is worsened by the presence of a mood disorder, such as depression or bipolar disorder).

After hearing about the different types of psychotic disorders, the patient's mom was seen by the hospital social worker and shared the following. At age eight, after his parents' separation, Winston saw the church pastor for "emotional outbursts" at school. He described the experience as traumatic, often being told, "Just pray to the Lord." At age twelve, it was reported he was seeing a therapist for five sessions for difficulty following the rules of his teachers and parents at home. At age seventeen, Winston visited the ER for a panic attack, insomnia, and passive thoughts of death. Voluntary hospitalization was recommended, but his mom objected and demanded that he was safe to come home. Since that time, she recalled hearing him state that he would never use any psychiatric medications and discussed his desire to stay away from "any poison." His parents further expressed significant concerns for his safety, gradual decline, bizarre behaviors, and disorganized thinking.

After three days of hospitalization and refusal to take medication or to attend any individual or group sessions, Winston was involuntarily committed to the hospital, and he was given the diagnosis of schizophrenia.

What is schizophrenia?

Schizophrenia is a persistent, long-lasting, and severe mental disorder that is characterized by the breakdown of thought or mind processes and difficulty understanding what is real. Schizophrenia does not imply and should not be confused with split personality or multiple personality disorder.[4] In many cases people suffering from the disorder fail to understand reality and cannot differentiate wrong from right. Many patients with schizophrenia experience confused thinking, lack of social engagement, false beliefs, hearing unreal voices, and lack of emotional expression. The condition of schizophrenia comes with additional mental disorders, and patients normally exhibit anxiety disorders, depression, and substance use difficulties.[5]

The exact cause is unknown, but research suggests that schizophrenia is caused by environmental and genetic factors, with symptoms typically starting in young adulthood. Schizophrenia affects 1 percent of the population but accounts for one-fourth of all mental health costs and takes up on average one in three psychiatric hospital beds. It is important to note that the prognosis of this disorder is varied at the individual level. It leads to a diminished life expectancy of twelve to fifteen years. Three-quarters of all schizophrenics smoke cigarettes, engage in little exercise, and are obese, and as many as 15 percent attempt suicide, which makes it their leading cause of death.[6] Because many schizophrenia patients are never able to work, they must be supported for life by Medicaid and other forms of public assistance. Despite the severity of diagnosis, only about half of all patients seek treatment in a given year. There remains an improving outlook for people with schizophrenia. Many experience recovery and lead independent, satisfying lives. Some factors that influence great prognosis include early treatment, abstinence from illicit drugs, prescribed medication compliance, and strong support systems.[7]

How is schizophrenia diagnosed?

Despite intensive research, no biological markers, lab tests, imaging studies, or physiological tests can be used to diagnose schizophrenia.[8] The diagnosis is carried out based on a psychiatric interview between a patient and the doctor. A structured series of questions are asked while aimed at finding out how the patient thinks. Background information sourced from relatives is also considered. Diagnosis requires ruling out other mental health illnesses and making sure that the illness is not based on substance abuse, medication, or a medical disorder.

What are common symptoms specific to schizophrenia?

The period before formal schizophrenia symptoms appear is known as the prodromal period, and these early-warning signs last about five years. The early signs of schizophrenia mostly happen in the teen years, and this can make them difficult to spot because these early signs are similar to behaviors often seen in teens in general. Symptoms may occur before the age of sixteen, but they may not become noticeable until between the ages of sixteen and thirty.[9]

The most common warning signs of schizophrenia include the following:[10]

Mood and emotional symptoms:

- Inability to cry or express joy (anhedonia)
- Feeling indifferent
- Feeling lonely and disconnected from self or others
- Severe anxiety, sadness, depression, anger, irritability, and rapid mood swings
- Hostility or suspiciousness
- Difficulty focusing and concentrating

Behavioral changes:

- Social withdrawal
- Deterioration of personal hygiene, clothing, and appearance
- Inappropriate laughter or crying
- Constant need to walk
- Increased craving for smoking cigarettes (70 to 90 percent smoke)
- Deterioration of academic or work performance

Cognitive changes:

- Disorganized talking and thinking among individuals when the disorder worsens
- Lost thoughts at times when patients experience schizophrenia and loosely connected spoken sentences with no meanings
- Trouble with social cues
- Extreme obsession with religion or occult(s)
- Lack of insight into the effect of their symptoms

Physical symptoms:

- Blank, flat, expressionless gaze or stare
- Oversleeping or insomnia
- Unusual gestures or postures
- Involuntary movements of tongue, mouth, and limbs (often a side effect of medications)

Not knowing what to do and blaming themselves, Winston's parents asked, "How did this happen? What did we do wrong?" The family was reassured that they did not cause schizophrenia, and causes, risk factors, treatment options, and prognosis were further explained.

What causes schizophrenia?

There are no definite causes of this disorder, but scientists have often attributed environment and genetics as sources of schizophrenia's development. Scientists believe that many different genes may increase the risk of schizophrenia, but no single gene causes the disorder by itself. It is not yet possible to use genetic information to predict who will develop schizophrenia. There is also no single laboratory test for schizophrenia. Brain chemicals that naturally occur include dopamine, serotonin, and glutamate neurotransmitters, and doctors ascertain that they can cause schizophrenia. Some experts also think that problems during brain development before birth may lead to faulty connections. The brain also undergoes major changes during puberty that could trigger psychotic symptoms in people who are vulnerable because of genetics or brain differences.

What are the risk factors, and who is affected?

In the United States, one person in one hundred, eighteen years and older, will develop schizophrenia during his or her lifetime.[11] The precise cause of schizophrenia is unknown, but certain factors seem to increase the risk of developing or triggering schizophrenia, including the following:

- **Family history/genetics:** The greatest single risk factor for developing schizophrenia is having a first-degree relative with the disease. For example, if one parent is affected, the risk is about 13 percent, and if both are affected, the risk is nearly 50 percent.[12]

Age and gender: The disorder affects males and females equally but tends to occur earlier in men. The age of onset for males tends to be in the late teens or early twenties. In contrast, women are generally affected in their twenties or early thirties. In rare instances, children as young as five can develop schizophrenia, and a sizable minority of female patients first become ill in middle or old age.[13]

Cultural and geographic factors: No cultural or geographic group is exempt from schizophrenia, although the course of the disease in developed countries seems to be more severe and an enormous economic burden.[14]

Race: Schizophrenia affects African Americans and Caucasians equally, yet African Americans are almost five times more likely to be diagnosed with schizophrenia compared with Caucasians admitted to state psychiatric hospitals.[15]

Environment: There are many environmental factors that have been linked to the development of schizophrenia, although none is considered a cause of the disorder. These include but are not limited to traumatic or highly stressful events in childhood, illicit drug use, maternal complications or illnesses during pregnancy, malnutrition during pregnancy, maternal exposure to the toxoplasmosis parasite, complications during birth, and being born during winter months.[16]

What are the treatment options?

The treatment of schizophrenia is lifelong and continues even when its symptoms have subsided. Antipsychotic medication is the first-line psychiatric treatment for schizophrenia and can reduce the acute symptoms of psychosis in about one to two weeks.[17] However, a combination of medications and psychosocial therapies is used to best manage the disorder long-term. There is no real cure for schizophrenia that exists, but many people with this disorder can live productive and fulfilling lives when proper treatment is administered to them. Psychosocial intervention treatment therapies are helpful to an individual, allowing one to recover the confidence and skills required to live a productive and self-reliant life in society. Case management helps people access facilities and regain skills that comprise employment, cleaning, cooking, budgeting, shopping, socializing, problem solving, and stress management.[18]

Medication treatment options. Atypical antipsychotics (second-generation medications) are newer and generally preferred because they pose a lower risk of severe side effects than conventional medications.

- **Examples:** Zyprexa (olanzapine), Seroquel (quetiapine), Risperdal (risperidone)
- **Common side effects:** weight gain, changes in metabolism (increases risk of diabetes and high cholesterol), sedation, low blood pressure

Typical antipsychotics (first generation) are older, cheaper, and well-studied.

- **Examples:** Haldol (haloperidol), Trilafon (perphenazine), Thorazine (chlorpromazine)
- **Common side effects:** rigidity, tremors, muscle spasms, restlessness, involuntary, repetitive body movements, electrocardiogram (EKG) changes

If medication is discontinued, the relapse rate is about 80 percent within two years. With continued drug treatment, only about 40 percent of recovered patients will suffer relapses.

Winston's symptoms improved with medication management and individual therapy. He was able to share events leading up to his arrest, which highlighted a clear prodromal period. He reported feeling very anxious in middle school and considered himself "shy and very smart." He reported writing two books on metaphysics in the seventh grade and was currently working on his third book on how to communicate with people in different dimensions. In high school he reported smoking marijuana "to focus" until it triggered a panic attack and the belief that the FBI was following him, a belief he still had. He denied any other history of alcohol or illicit drug use. He reported losing interest in classes at his university and became very active in a local black advocacy group, where he attempted to organize several rallies to address discrimination and recent shootings of unarmed black men. He reported that members expressed concerns but that "Doc, they were just haters."

He was discharged to an intensive outpatient treatment program that highlighted a holistic treatment approach. He currently attends weekly individual therapy and groups. He was seen by a vocational counselor and volunteers at a soup kitchen. His parents became very active in the National Alliance on Mental Illness (NAMI) and conducted several workshops at their local church, sorority, and NAACP chapter. They also started marriage counseling and individual therapy. Despite improvement, Winston remained unsure about his diagnosis and compliance with medications long-term but plans to stay committed because "it makes me sleep and have good dreams."

Knowledge Is Power: When to Seek Help

It is advised that anyone with an acute change in mental status (a noticeable change in mood or behavior), whether diagnosed with schizophrenia or not, should be taken to a hospital or physician for evaluation. Seeking help early prevents complications that can come with the disorder and further improves recovery chances. Seeking help enables proper treatment and support that further reduces symptoms, and people can work independently, build satisfying relationships, and enjoy good lives. There's no sure way to prevent schizophrenia. However, early treatment may help to get symptoms under control and may contribute to improving the disease's long-term outlook.[19] Sticking with the treatment plan can help prevent relapses or worsening of schizophrenia symptoms.

Notes

1. "Early Psychosis and Psychosis," National Alliance on Mental Health, accessed, https://www.nami.org/earlypsychosis.
2. American Psychiatric Association, *Diagnostic and Statistical Manual of Mental* Disorders, 5th ed. (Washington, DC: American Psychiatric Association, 2013).
3. "Think You're Going Crazy? A Beginner's Guide to Psychosis," Elana Miller, Zen Psychiatry, October 20, 2011, http://zenpsychiatry.com/beginners-guide-to-psychosis/.
4. Marco M. Picchioni and Robin Murray, "Schizophrenia," *BMJ* 335, no. 7610 (2007): 91–5.
5. "Schizophrenia," National Institute of Mental Illness, accessed January 12, 2018, https://www.nimh.nih.gov/health/topics/schizophrenia/index.shtml.
6. Hiram Joseph Wildgust, Richard Hodgson, and Mike Beary, "The Paradox of Premature Mortality in Schizophrenia: New Research Questions," *Journal of Psychopharmacology* 24, no. 4 (2010): 9–15.
7. "Schizophrenia Facts and Statistics," The Internet Mental Health Initiative, accessed January 12, 2018, http://www.schizophrenia.com/szfacts.htm.
8. Stephen M. Lawrie, Bayanne Olabi, Jeremy Hall, and Andrew M. McIntosh, "Do We Have Any Solid Evidence of Clinical Utility about the Pathophysiology of Schizophrenia?" *World Psychiatry* 10, no. 1 (2011): 19–31.
9. "Psychosis (Schizophrenia) in Children and Youth," Mental Health America, accessed January 12, 2018, http://www.mentalhealthamerica.net/conditions/psychosis-schizophrenia-children-and-youth.
10. "The Causes of Schizophrenia," Schizophrenia.com, accessed January 12, 2018, http://schizophrenia.com/hypo.php.

11. "Schizophrenia," National Institute of Mental Health, accessed January 12, 2018, https://www.nimh.nih.gov/health/topics/schizophrenia/index.shtml.

12. Barbara Burns McGrath and Karen L. Edwards, "When Family Means More (or Less) Than Genetics: The Intersection of Culture, Family, and Genomics," *Journal of Transcultural Nursing* 20, no. 3 (2009): 270–77.

13. Stephen H. Schultz, Stephen W. North, and Cleveland G. Shields, "Schizophrenia: A Review," *American Family Physician* 75, no. 12 (2007): 1821–29.

14. Heuy Yi Chong, Siew Li Teoh, David Bin-Chia Wu, Surachai Kotirium, Chiun-Fang Chiou, and Nathorn Chaiyakunapruk, "Global Economic Burden of Schizophrenia: A Systematic Review," *Neuropsychiatric Disease and Treatment* 12 (2016): 357–73.

15. Robert C. Schwartz and David M. Blankenship, "Racial Disparities in Psychotic Disorder Diagnosis: A Review of Empirical Literature," *World Journal of Psychiatry* 4, no. 4 (2014): 133–40.

16. Kimberlie Dean and Robin M. Murray, "Environmental Risk Factors for Psychosis," *Dialogues in Clinical Neuroscience* 7, no. 1 (2005): 69–80.

17. "Pharmacotherapy for Schizophrenia: Acute and Maintenance Phase Treatment," T. Scott Stroup and Stephen Marder, UpToDate, last updated May 23, 2017, https://www.uptodate.com/contents/pharmacotherapy-for-schizophrenia-acute-and-maintenance-phase-treatment.

18. John M. Kane and Christoph U. Correll, "Pharmacologic Treatment of Schizophrenia," *Dialogues in Clinical Neuroscience* 12, no. 3 (2010): 345–57.

19. "The Importance of Early Treatment for Schizophrenia and Psychosis," Schizophrenia.com, May 8, 2014, accessed January 12, 2018, http://schizophrenia.com/?p=406.

CHAPTER 7

Substance Use Disorders and Addiction

Why Won't They Just Quit?
TIMOTHY BENSON, MD

Xavier is an eighteen-year-old college student who was home for summer vacation. During the week, he worked at a local grocery store, and he hung out with his friends on the weekends. Since his return from school, his parents noticed that when he was not working, Xavier spent much of his time at home playing video games and smoking marijuana. They had told him to stop and threatened to kick him out of the house. His reply to their demands was commonly, "Don't worry; I don't have a problem, and besides, it's legal now." As the summer progressed, he began to smoke more often, starting earlier in the day. He had made several attempts to try to stop, but each time he resumed smoking after a few days. At work he began to show up late and take long, extended breaks. Several employees complained that sometimes he smelled like marijuana. His boss warned him several times about the complaints and his absences. After several weeks of declining performance, Xavier was let go. Instead of finding a new job, he spent most days at home in the basement alone playing video games and smoking marijuana.

Do you know someone like Xavier? Does he really have a problem, or is this normal behavior, especially for college students? Does it matter whether it is legal or not? What should his parents do or say? Is kicking him out of the house the best way to deal with this matter? These and many other questions are common when it comes to the topic of drugs and alcohol. It's not always easy to know when to be concerned or what to do about it. In this chapter you will learn multiple aspects of addiction: how it is defined, what signs to look for, and how it is treated. Let's take a closer look.

What does it mean to have an addiction?

According to the National Institute on Drug Abuse (NIDA), addiction is defined as a chronic, relapsing brain disease that is characterized by compulsive drug seeking and use, despite harmful consequences.[1] What this means is that an individual who has an addiction has an extremely strong desire for drugs or alcohol, so much so that they will go to great lengths to obtain it and will continue to use it despite how many problems their use causes. Because drinking alcohol is common in our society and the majority of people who drink or use drugs don't become alcoholics or addicts, how do you really know when there is a problem?

To answer this question, the *Diagnostic and Statistical Manual of Mental Disorders* (*DSM-5*), the book that characterizes all psychiatric disorders, describes the specific criteria for having an addiction. Of note, in the *DSM-5*, addictions are now referred to as substance use disorders (SUD). A brief summary of the criteria follows:

- Drinking or using more than what was planned
- Multiple unsuccessful attempts at trying to stop or cut down use
- Spending a lot of time thinking about using drugs or how to get them
- Having strong cravings or desires to use
- Failing responsibilities at work, home, or school because of use
- Continuing to use despite the problems it's causing
- Stopping or cutting down on important social, work, or recreational activities
- Continuing to use in dangerous situations

- Continuing to use despite frequent physical or psychological problems caused by use
- Needing more and more alcohol or drugs to have a similar effect
- Experiencing withdrawal symptoms when use has stopped

If the individual has two or three of these symptoms, then the addiction or substance use disorder is considered mild. However, having four or five of these symptoms would be considered moderate, and having six or seven would be considered severe.[2]

It is also important to know that an addiction is not only associated with the use of substances. The same criteria have also been used in the assessment of what are called behavioral addictions, including gambling, shopping, video games, Internet use, sex, and overeating, to name a few.[3]

How serious is the problem of drugs?

It's pretty serious. In fact, in this country alone, we spend over an estimated $740 billion annually on all costs (crime, health care, lost work productivity) related to tobacco, drug, and alcohol abuse. To give you an idea of the scope of the problem, here are some important statistics:[4]

- Approximately 21.5 million people aged twelve or older had a substance use disorder in the past year.
- In 2016 there were over 64,000 deaths due to drug overdose. That's an average of 175 deaths per day.
- Over five million emergency room visits per year are drug related.
- Rates of illicit drug use are highest among those aged eighteen to twenty-five.

What's the most common addiction?

Although marijuana is the most commonly abused illicit drug in the United States, the most common addiction is to tobacco (nicotine). It is estimated that one out of every five adults and teenagers smoke. It's not only the most common addiction but also the most deadly. According to the surgeon general's report, cigarette smoking is responsible for more than 480,000 deaths per year in the United States, including more than 41,000 deaths resulting from secondhand smoke exposure. This is about one in five deaths annually, or 1,300 deaths every day.[5, 6]

Do substance use disorders affect African Americans differently?

First let's touch briefly on the rates of drug and alcohol use between African Americans and the majority population. According to the 2014 National Survey on Drug Use and Health, despite what might be portrayed in the media, African Americans are less likely to abuse alcohol than the majority population, 17.3 percent versus 22.8 percent, respectively. In this survey, African Americans did have a slightly higher percentage of illicit drug use, 12.4 percent versus the national average of 10.2 percent. However, the most significant differences were not in rates of use but rather in the severity of the health consequences. African Americans with substance use disorders were more likely to experience higher death rates, be victims of crimes, experience higher alcohol-related problems, and contract HIV/AIDS.[7]

How does someone become addicted?

Addiction can happen to anyone regardless of socioeconomic status and may be influenced by biology, environment, and/or stage of development.[8] This is important to realize because many people are under the impression that it is based on a moral choice. Labeling someone with an addiction as "bad" is not helpful and is often counterproductive. However, understanding the risks that make someone susceptible to becoming an addict gives us a better chance at developing effective strategies for treatment. Let's take a look at the most common factors that place one at risk:

- **Family history:** Studies have shown that a child with one alcoholic parent has a 50 to 60 percent greater chance of becoming an alcoholic compared to children without alcoholic parents.
- **Environment:** Poverty, parental neglect, having friends who use or drink (peer pressure), or having a history of trauma increases the risk.
- **Other mental disorders:** Half of those with a drug or alcohol addiction also have depression, anxiety, or bipolar disorder.
- **Type of drug:** Cocaine, heroin, and methamphetamines are more addictive than alcohol or marijuana.
- **Early use:** Over 90 percent of those with an addiction began drinking, smoking, or using illicit drugs before the age of eighteen.
- **Method of use:** Drugs that are inhaled or injected can be more addictive because they enter the bloodstream quicker.

The presence of these risk factors does not mean that one will automatically develop an addiction. However, the odds are greater for social or frequent use to progress into a full addiction the more risk factors that are present.

Does having a six-pack of beer at a barbecue mean there's a problem?

Because alcohol is so much a part of the American culture, it may be hard to determine the difference between normal and abnormal drinking. Abnormal is always relative and is based on multiple factors, including context and history. One may think that there is a difference between getting intoxicated at a football game once a week versus frequently getting tipsy on lunch breaks. However, it may not be that simple to determine which one might have a problem. In order to help make it clearer, the National Institute on Alcohol Abuse and Alcoholism (NIAAA) has set up guidelines for what is considered at-risk or heavy drinking. For instance, heavy drinking for men is defined as having more than four drinks on a given day or more than fourteen drinks per week. Heavy drinking for women is having more than three drinks on any day or more than seven drinks per week.[9] It's important to know that what is considered a drink depends not only on the amount but also on the type of alcohol. In the United States, a standard drink is equal to the following:

- Twelve-ounce can of beer
- Five-ounce cup of wine
- Eight to nine ounces of malt liquor
- One and a half ounces of distilled spirits (vodka, gin, rum, etc.)

How can some people drink or use drugs but never become addicted?

As previously stated, the overwhelming majority of people who drink or use drugs recreationally will never become addicted. For instance, prior reports indicate that only 9 percent of those using marijuana will become dependent on it. However, more recent data suggest that up to 30 percent of those who use marijuana may have some degree of marijuana use disorder.[10, 11] Although we know the factors that place one at a greater risk, it doesn't fully explain how the transition is made from occasional use to dependence. Some answers may be found in our biological makeup. There is mounting evidence in brain research suggesting that those who have a greater likelihood of becoming addicted have brains that experience a drug in a different way than those who are not addicted. Researchers have found that brain scans light up differently in addicts than they do in nonaddicted patients.[12] What this suggests is that they may feel a greater intensity from the effect of the drug, which may lead to a stronger desire to repeat use.

What signs do I look for if I think someone is using?

The warning signs of addiction or recent use can be physical, emotional, or behavioral in nature. Physically there may be signs of shakiness, dilated pupils, frequent sniffling or runny nose, vomiting, decreased coordination, or difficulty sleeping. Emotional signs may appear as paranoia, frequent mood swings, irritability, excessive excitement, or hallucinations. Certain behaviors may also increase suspicion. These include isolating at home, increased aggression, relationship problems, taking major risks, spending a lot of money, neglecting responsibilities, or having problems at school or work, to name a few.

How do health-care professionals determine if someone is at risk?

Primary care health professionals often play an essential role in helping an individual start the process of getting treatment. In the office setting, several questionnaires can be used to screen for those who may be at risk. For instance, a common one specific to alcohol abuse is the CAGE questionnaire. The four questions include (1) "Do you feel the need to Cut back on the amount you are drinking?" This question helps to determine if individuals have been struggling with trying to stop or slow down. (2) "Are people Annoyed by the amount you are drinking?" What may seem normal to the individual may actually be of concern to others around them. It may be easier for one to acknowledge that others are worried than to admit to having a problem. (3) "Do you feel Guilty at times about how much you drink?" In some instances the individual may be worried about his or her drinking but won't open up about it unless asked. (4) "Do you have a drink as an Eye-opener in the morning?" This question not only helps to determine the frequency of drinking but also the severity. Drinking early in the morning may indicate an attempt to avoid withdrawal symptoms. A yes to any one of these questions does not necessarily indicate that there is an addiction, but rather it suggests the need for further exploration on drinking behaviors.

Is it OK to say no even if I see him or her struggling or in pain?

One of the biggest challenges in dealing with a loved one who may be suffering from an addiction is figuring out how to best help him or her. The most difficult thing to do may be to set a limit by saying no. Whether it is denying requests for money when you suspect it may be going toward drug use or refusing to constantly bail the person out of trouble, there can be a tremendous amount of guilt associated with taking a hard stand.

It is important to know that continuing to enable someone, no matter how heartfelt the plea, is not likely going to help in the long run. Constantly giving in can likely prolong the process of getting appropriate help and may make things worse. One helpful point is to learn the difference between enabling and empowering someone. In essence, enabling refers to the things you do that allow current behaviors to continue as is—for example, making excuses for someone who is behaving poorly or neglecting responsibilities. On the other hand, to empower someone is to help the person build the confidence and skills to handle his or her own problems—for example, supporting him or her to get treatment. What truly differentiates enabling versus empowering is one word: responsibility. If you are concerned that you might be enabling someone, just ask yourself the question: Does my action or decision require the person to take more responsibility for his or her actions or help him or her avoid responsibility?

What can I do about it?

If you are or a loved one is suspected of suffering from a substance use disorder, the best thing to do is to seek treatment. Delaying treatment can make the problem bigger by affecting one's ability to function now and in the future. Untreated addictions that lead to long-term use can cause changes in brain chemicals and circuits that affect learning, judgment, decision making, stress, memory, and behavior.[13] Therefore, it is important to seek help sooner rather than later. Fortunately, treatment is readily available, although it is not used as often as it should be. It has been shown that one out of ten individuals who need treatment actually receives it. It is also important to note that the rates for African Americans receiving treatment are approximately one-third of the rates of treatment for the majority population.[14]

To make matters worse, a major treatment opportunity is often missed in our justice system. According to the National Center on Addiction and

Substance Abuse, 65 percent of prisoners in state and federal prison meet criteria for substance use disorders, but only 11 percent of them receive treatment during incarceration. An estimated 650,000 inmates are released yearly without treatment. That's 650,000 missed opportunities to help people get better. Untreated addictions are also what contribute to high rates of return to prison.[15]

How are addictions treated?

There are numerous ways for the person with a substance use disorder to get help. The primary settings for addiction treatment are separated into three categories: inpatient, residential, and outpatient. Inpatient treatment is when a person with an addiction or other psychiatric condition is treated in the hospital setting. Overnight stays can range from a few days or weeks depending on how serious the problem. This is usually appropriate in emergency situations when someone has overdosed or is at an extreme medical risk. In the case of someone who has been addicted to alcohol or benzodiazepines, a detoxification period is often required. What this means is that physicians prescribe specific medications to gradually allow the body to safely adapt to the absence of alcohol. To abruptly stop alcohol can place someone at risk for seizures or what is called delirium tremens (DTs), causing significant instability in the nervous system and blood pressures, which could eventually result in death.

Similar to the inpatient setting is what is called residential treatment. This refers to a treatment facility, often outside of a hospital setting, where patients stay for longer periods of time. A typical residential stay is about thirty days. Residential treatments can be extremely helpful because they provide an opportunity for the individual to completely get out of the demands of his or her normal daily life and to enter a completely supportive environment so that he or she can focus solely on healing and learning.

The outpatient treatment setting includes individual and group therapies or self-help groups. There is also what is referred to as intensive outpatient programs (IOPs), which are often the next step after a detox or inpatient hospitalization. An IOP usually consists of three to four hours a day for several days per week of addiction and mental health education in a group- or classroom-style format. The primary foci in IOPs are coping skills training and relapse prevention. This format can occur during the day or evenings, which can be helpful to those who need a high level of structured support but are not able to take off a lot of time from work or school.

How does therapy work for addictions?

There are several psychological components to a substance use disorder. Therefore, there are different types of therapy that provide multiple ways of approaching treatment. Some therapies focus on helping people manage their emotions. Some therapies focus on helping the clients to understand the connection between their thoughts and addictive behaviors. Others are geared toward helping a person gain the motivation or confidence to quit the habit. The main goal of many of these individual therapies is to enhance skills and develop strategies that will not only prevent relapses but also will help the individual to work toward a healthy, sober lifestyle.

For those who may not feel comfortable with individual therapy, group therapy can be a powerful alternative. Groups are primarily led by a trained clinician and consist of two or more individuals who meet on a regular basis to get support and to discuss challenges related to their addictions. The benefits of group therapy are the increased amount of support and the ability to learn from others who are going through similar challenges. If cost is an issue, self-help groups can provide a great first step toward getting help. Such organizations as Alcoholic Anonymous (AA), Narcotics Anonymous (NA), and Self-Management and Recovery Therapy (SMART) groups are free and provide a tremendous amount of support. The only requirement for participation in these groups is that the individual have a *desire* to stop using.

Does a relapse mean that treatment has failed?

No. The treatment of addictions is a process, and relapses are a part of the process. Rarely does the journey to a healthy, sober lifestyle proceed in a straight line. In early recovery, three steps forward are often accompanied by two steps back. The key to effective treatment is for one not to lose hope but to continue to build coping skills and confidence along the way. Therefore, relapses are not to be judged or punished; they are to be understood. Gaining insight into the factors that led to the relapse will allow one to modify strategies in a way that helps to avoid such pitfalls in the future. Despite setbacks, the focus should remain on continuing in the treatment process.

Why won't they just stop?

There are multiple reasons that can make it difficult to stop drinking alcohol or using drugs. First we must look at the level of motivation. People may not stop because they don't feel they have a problem, or they may recognize they have a problem but don't feel ready to completely give it up.

Sometimes people keep using because they may be struggling with depression, bipolar disorder, or anxiety. Using drugs or alcohol to manage emotions is often referred to as self-medicating.

In other instances it may be difficult to stop using because of severe withdrawal effects. Especially when it comes to alcohol, stopping abruptly after long, consistent periods of heavy drinking can result in significant withdrawal tremors, hallucinations, seizures, and in some cases, death. Again, this is why it is highly recommended that heavy drinkers get safely detoxed in facilities that have access to appropriate medical care.

Are there medications that work for addictions?

The most effective treatments for addictions are those that help address both the physical and the psychological hold that an addiction can have on a person. Medications can help supplement the treatment process but are seldom effective on their own. Which medications would be most helpful can depend on the type of addiction the person has. Here are a few examples of how some medications work to treat addictions:

- Reduce withdrawal symptoms (buprenorphine, suboxone, benzo-diazapines)
- Reduce the pleasurable effects of drugs or alcohol (naltrexone)
- Increase negative effects of alcohol (disulfiram)
- Reduce cravings (acamprosate, naltrexone, varenicline)
- Treat other psychiatric conditions that affect the likelihood of sub-stance use (antidepressants and antianxiety medications)

It is worth noting that some of the most effective forms of treatment combine both medication and therapy. A common protocol of the most successful treatments often include the following:[16]

1. Detoxification: the process by which the body rids itself of a drug
2. Behavioral counseling
3. Medication (for opioid, tobacco, or alcohol addiction)
4. Evaluation and treatment for co-occurring mental health issues, such as depression and anxiety
5. Long-term follow up to prevent relapse

Addictions or substance use disorders affect many people in this country, and they do not discriminate. No matter one's status in life, addictions can occur and have a major effect on the individual and his or her family. Although it is not entirely clear how addictions to drugs or alcohol develop, there are a multitude of factors that can put one at risk. It is true that effective treatment is available, but unfortunately, the available resources are not used often enough. If you are or a loved one is struggling with an addiction, reach out for support. Find the type of treatment that works best for you, but just get help. Realize that the road to living a healthy, sober lifestyle is never a straight one. It may take some time, and there may be many ups and downs, but in the end it will be worth it because you are worth it. Just remember that no matter how hard it gets, stick with it and take it one day at a time.

Notes

1. "Drugs, Brains, and Behavior: The Science of Addiction," National Institute on Drug Abuse, accessed January 15, 2018, https://www.drugabuse.gov/publications/drugs-brains-behavior-science-addiction.

2. American Psychiatric Association, *Diagnostic and Statistical Manual of Mental Disorders*, 5th ed. (Washington, DC: American Psychiatric Association, 2013).

3. Seyyed Salman Alavi, Masoud Ferdosi, Fereshte Jannatifard, Mehdi Eslami, Hamed Alaghemandan, and Mehrdad Setare, "Behavioral Addiction versus Substance Addiction: Correspondence of Psychiatric and Psychological Views," *International Journal of Preventive Medicine* 3, no. 4 (2012): 290–94.

4. "Trends & Statistics," National Institute on Drug Abuse, accessed January 15, 2018, https://www.drugabuse.gov/related-topics/trends-statistics.

5. US Department of Health and Human Services, *The Health Consequences of Smoking—50 Years of Progress: A Report of the Surgeon General* (Rockville, MD: US Department of Health and Human Services, 2014).

6. Prabhat Jha Chinthanie Ramasundarahettige, Victoria Landsman, Brian Rostron, Michael Thun, Robert Anderson, Tim McAfee, and Richard Peto, "21st Century Hazards of Smoking and Benefits of Cessation in the United States," *New England Journal of Medicine* 368 (2013): 341–50.

7. Center for Behavioral Health Statistics and Quality, *Behavioral Health Trends in the United States: Results from the 2014 National Survey on Drug Use and Health* (Rockville, MD: Center for Behavioral Health Statistics and Quality, Substance Abuse and Mental Health Services Administration, 2015).

8. "Understanding Drug Use and Addiction," National Institute on Drug Abuse, accessed January 15, 2018, https://www.drugabuse.gov/publications/drugfacts/understanding-drug-use-addiction.

9. National Institute on Alcohol Abuse and Alcoholism, "NIAAA Council Approves Definition of Binge Drinking," *NIAAA Newsletter* 3 (Winter 2004): 3.

10. Deborah S. Hasin, Tulshi D. Saha, Bradley T. Kerridge, Risë B. Goldstein, S. Patricia Chou, Haitao Zhang, Jeesun Jung, et al., "Prevalence of Marijuana Use Disorders in the United States between 2001–2002 and 2012–2013," *JAMA Psychiatry* 72, no. 12 (2015): 1235–42.

11. Alan J. Budney, Roger Roffman, Robert S. Stephens, and Denise Walker, "Marijuana Dependence and Its Treatment," *Addiction Science & Clinical Practice* 4, no. 1 (2007): 4–16.

12. Joanna S. Fowler, Nora D. Volkow, Cheryl A. Kassed, and Linda Chang, "Imaging the Addicted Human Brain," *Science & Practice Perspectives* 3, no. 2 (2007): 4–16.

13. "Understanding Drug Use and Addiction," National Institute on Drug Abuse, accessed January 15, 2018, https://www.drugabuse.gov/publications/drugfacts/understanding-drug-use-addiction.

14. "Treatment Statistics," National Institute on Drug Abuse, accessed January 7, 2018, https://www.drugabuse.gov/publications/drugfacts/treatment-statistics.

15. National Center on Addiction and Substance Abuse at Columbia University, *Behind Bars II: Substance Abuse and America's Prison Population* (New York: National Center on Addiction and Substance Abuse at Columbia University, 2010).

16. "Treatment Approaches for Drug Addiction," National Institute on Drug Abuse, accessed January 15, 2018, https://www.drugabuse.gov/publications/drugfacts/treatment-approaches-drug-addiction.

CHAPTER 8
Childhood Disorders

Won't a Belt Handle That?
MICHAEL PRATTS, MD

There are approximately ten million African American children in the United States today. One out of every five of our children will experience an emotional problem each year. About half of all mental conditions begin by age fourteen.[1] According to the American Academy of Pediatrics, the breakdown of mental disorders is 8 percent for attention deficit hyperactivity disorder, 4 percent for mood disorders, 2 percent for conduct disorder, 1 percent for anxiety, and 1 percent for eating disorders. Boys had 2.1 times greater prevalence of attention deficit hyperactivity disorder than girls, girls had twofold higher rates of mood disorders than boys, and there were no gender differences in the rates of anxiety disorders or conduct disorder. Only approximately one half of those with one of the disorders assessed had sought treatment with a mental health professional.[2]

We will review the most to the least common reasons for mental health referrals and discuss important questions that parents should be prepared to ask during the evaluation process. Most diagnosis in adults also occurs in children. We purposely left out diagnoses that are covered elsewhere in the book to avoid repetition.

Behavior Disorders

Attention deficit hyperactivity disorder. The most commonly diagnosed condition in children, attention deficit hyperactivity disorder (ADHD) affects approximately six million children in the United States. It is usually brought to the attention of parents or caregivers once a child starts school, day care, or some other routine setting where the child is around other kids and an observer notices that the child's behavior is significantly different from that of other children in the group. By comparison to the group, children with ADHD will be far more active or inattentive or both. This observation only becomes more evident over time. Teachers or day care workers will point this out to parents, prompting a visit to the pediatrician. You should know there are no blood tests, brain scans, or genetic tests currently for ADHD.

ADHD comes from brain chemistry imbalance. This imbalance results in children and adults displaying a typical set of behaviors as described in the *Diagnostic and Statistical Manual of Mental Disorders (DSM-5)*. Children must meet criteria for inattention or hyperactivity/impulsivity or both.

- **Inattention:** Six or more of these symptoms must be present for at least six months, be inconsistent with the child's developmental level, and have a negative effect on his or her social and academic activities. The following must occur often:
  - Fails to pay close attention to details
  - Has trouble sustaining attention
  - Doesn't seem to listen when spoken to directly
  - Fails to follow through on instructions and finish schoolwork or chores
  - Has trouble getting organized
  - Avoids or dislikes doing things that require sustained focus or thinking
  - Loses things frequently
  - Is easily distracted by other things
  - Forgets things

- **Hyperactivity and impulsivity:** Six or more of these symptoms must be present for at least six months, be inconsistent with the child's developmental level, and have a negative effect on his or her social and academic activities. The following must occur often:
    - Fidgets with hands or feet or squirms in chair
    - Frequently leaves chair when seating is expected
    - Runs or climbs excessively
    - Has trouble playing or engaging in activities quietly
    - Acts on-the-go or as if driven by a motor
    - Talks excessively
    - Blurts out answers before questions are completed
    - Has trouble waiting or taking turns
    - Interrupts or intrudes on what others are doing

Initial evaluations will usually consist of a review of the child's basic health status, diet, medications, and major changes in the child's life. The behavioral history should be the focus. Bring with you any documentation from teachers or care providers to help further aid in the evaluation. In addition, parents should be asked to complete a rating scale for assessing ADHD. It should be noted that these questions are subjective, and inaccurate reporting by parents and/or teachers can influence the results.

If at this point your child is still suspected of having ADHD and you feel that ADHD may be the cause of your child's struggles, a trial intervention should be recommended. You should know that there is no cure for ADHD; however, there are many treatment options. These options include behavior therapy, medications, and school accommodations.

The goals of behavior therapy are to learn or strengthen positive behaviors and to eliminate unwanted or problem behaviors. Behavior therapy includes training for parents, behavior therapy with children, or a combination. Teachers also use behavior therapy to help reduce problem behaviors at school.

Medication options can be divided into two broad categories: stimulants and nonstimulants. The most common type of medication used for treating ADHD is called a stimulant. Although it may seem unusual to treat hyperactivity with a medication that is a stimulant, it works because it increases the brain chemicals dopamine and norepinephrine, which are low and essential for concentration, focus, and attention. Stimulants work right away, the same day, and don't need to build up.

Under medical supervision, stimulant medications are safe. As with any medication, there are risks and possible side effects. For example, stimulants can raise blood pressure and heart rate. Therefore, a child with any health problems should inform the prescriber before taking a stimulant. The most common side effects from stimulants are decreased appetite, difficulty falling asleep, tics (sudden, repetitive movements or sounds), increased anxiety or irritability, stomach pain, or headaches.

The more common nonstimulant medications include atomoxetine (Strattera), bupropion (Wellbutrin), guanfacine (Intuniv), and clonidine (Catapres). Unlike stimulants that work immediately, these medications may take days to weeks to take effect.

Are black boys overdiagnosed with ADHD?

It is commonly stated in the black community that black males are over diagnosed with ADHD. This statement can be true and not true at the same time. Hyperactivity and inattentiveness are symptoms of ADHD, but they are not specific to ADHD. Inattentiveness and hyperactivity may be seen in other mental and physical health issues. The most common misdiagnosis is another mental health issue, such as mood and anxiety disorders. Also, behavioral issues in children who are frequently misdiagnosed are family conflict, poor nutrition, inadequate sleep, or other learning disorders or disabilities. Exposure to drugs, cigarettes, or alcohol while the mother was pregnant often lead to ADHD-like symptoms as well.[3]

Black boys on average are less likely to be diagnosed with ADHD than their white male counterparts. Black males are more likely to be diagnosed with opposition defiant disorder and conduct disorder, which are typically less treatable and often require structured environments leading to harsher disciplinary issues, including in-school suspension, expulsion, and even incarceration into juvenile services. Being placed out of the classroom means less instructional days in school. The amount of days in class has a direct effect on the ability to pass a grade level and on dropout rates. Nearly 60 percent of black males who do not complete high school will be incarcerated. This missed and underdiagnosed ADHD continues to have a major effect on black homes, families, and communities.[4]

Childhood trauma often leads to ADHD symptoms. Within all races nationally, approximately one in four girls and one in six boys before the age of eighteen will be sexually molested, raped, or abused.[5] Black children are more often survivors of community violence and individual, public, academic, and institutional racism.[6] This is often seen in unclean air and water, public policy, lack of funding of educational systems, over- and under policing, and inadequate nutrition (food deserts).[7] Despite these issues, many children in these affected communities do quite well. Some examples include access to extended family members, doing well academically, mentoring programs, social services, sports, and exposure to positive role models and activities.[8]

Oppositional defiant disorder. Every child can be oppositional at times. Talking back, disobeying, challenging authority, and arguing are normal behaviors on occasion. For early adolescents and two-, three-, and four-year-olds, this behavior is expected. This behavior can be worse when the child is hungry, tired, or upset. When this behavior is so frequent or out of proportion to other children of similar age, consider the diagnosis of oppositional defiant disorder (ODD).

DSM-5 criteria for diagnosis of ODD show a pattern of behavior that

- includes at least four symptoms from any of these categories: angry and irritable mood, argumentative and defiant behavior, or vindictiveness;
- occurs with at least one individual who is not a sibling;
- causes significant problems at work, school, or home;
- occurs on its own rather than as part of the course of another mental health problem, such as a substance use disorder, depression, or bipolar disorder; and
- lasts at least six months.

DSM-5 criteria for diagnosis of ODD include both emotional and behavioral symptoms.

Angry and irritable mood:

- Often loses temper
- Is often touchy or easily annoyed by others
- Is often angry and resentful

Argumentative and defiant behavior:

- Often argues with adults or people in authority
- Often actively defies or refuses to comply with adults' requests or rules
- Often deliberately annoys people
- Often blames others for his or her mistakes or misbehavior

Vindictiveness:

- Is often spiteful or vindictive
- Has shown spiteful or vindictive behavior at least twice in the past six months

These behaviors must be displayed more often than is typical for your child's peers. For children younger than five, the behavior must occur on most days during a period of at least six months. For children five or older, the behavior must occur at least once a week for at least six months.

There is no medication approved for ODD. Treatment consists of assembling an effective support group of parents, teachers, and peers. Individual psychotherapy is recommended.

Conduct disorder. One of the more serious and disappointing conditions for parents is conduct disorder (CD). Children with this diagnosis can display violent behavior, break laws, intentionally hurt others and/or animals, set fires, destroy property, force children into sexual acts, and steal. It is not uncommon for children and adolescents to have an occasional behavioral problem; however, when this behavior is long-lasting, represents a pattern, and causes significant disruption is the child's life, conduct disorder should be considered. According to the DSM-5, to diagnose conduct disorder, least four of the following must be present:

- Aggressive behavior toward others and animals
- Frequent physical altercations with others
- Use of a weapon to harm others
- Deliberately physically cruel to other people
- Deliberately physically cruel to animals
- Involvement in confrontational economic-order crime, such as mugging
- Perpetration of a forcible sex act on another
- Property destruction by arson
- Property destruction by other means
- Engagement in nonconfrontational economic-order crime, such as breaking and entering
- Engagement in nonconfrontational retail theft, such as shoplifting
- Disregard of parents' curfew prior to age thirteen
- Has run away from home at least two times
- Has been truant before age thirteen

These behaviors cause significant impairment in functioning.

There is no medication approved for conduct disorder. Treatment consists of assembling an effective support group of parents, teachers, and peers. Individual psychotherapy is recommended.

Depression in children. More commonly considered a condition for adults, children and teenagers may also develop depression. We diagnose it as an illness when it persists and interferes with the child's ability to function. According to the American Academy of Child and Adolescent Psychiatry, "About 5 percent of children and adolescents suffer from depression at any given point in time. Children under stress, who experience loss, or who have attention, learning, conduct or anxiety disorders are at a higher risk for depression. Depression also tends to run in families."[9] What makes this a less straightforward diagnosis is that the behavior of depressed children varies greatly from child to child, and teenagers may differ from the behavior of depressed adults.

The symptoms of childhood depression include frequent sadness; tearfulness; crying; decreased interest in activities or inability to enjoy previously enjoyable activities; hopelessness; excessive boredom; complaints of low energy; withdrawing from friends/social isolation; guilt; heightened sensitivity to rejection or failure; an increase in irritability, anger, or hostility; more frequent complaints of physical illnesses, such as headaches and stomachaches; decline in school performance; poor concentration; increase or decrease in eating and/or sleeping patterns; and thoughts or expressions of suicide.

Depressed children are at increased risk for committing suicide. Depressed adolescents may use alcohol or other drugs to try to feel better. Depressed kids may hurt themselves to feel better; this seems very strange to most people. Individuals may feel so bad that they lose feelings altogether. This loss of feeling or feeling numb is so uncomfortable that pain from self-injury is preferable to no feeling at all. Kids may make superficial cuts on their arms, legs, or stomachs. Kids may rub their skin very hard to cause a burn or use fire to burn themselves. This self-injurious behavior is not considered suicidal behavior. A significant change in behavior or attitude, such as decreased personal hygiene and socializing or losing interest in things that were thought interesting, may be a sign of depression. Many children don't just become sad or depressed like adults do, so parents and teachers may not realize that what they are seeing is depression. Given the difficulty that young people have with self-reflection, when asked directly, many of these children are unable to identify that they are in fact depressed.

The good news is that there are treatments for depression. Both individual and family therapy are recommended first. For example, cognitive behavioral therapy (CBT) and interpersonal psychotherapy (IPT) are forms of individual therapy shown to be effective in treating depression. Treatment may also include the use of antidepressant medication.

Disruptive mood dysregulation disorder. Disruptive mood dysregulation disorder (DMDD) is a childhood condition representing "temper tantrums" that are extreme and greatly out of proportion to the inciting event. Children with this condition usually are fine if left alone doing what they prefer or when playing as long as they are winning or things are going their way. Once told no, any attempt at redirections away from their preference, or losing a game, they become highly agitated, fly into a rage, destroy property, and become physically aggressive, hitting, kicking, biting, or even using items as weapons. Parents usually describe the child during these "rage attacks" as inconsolable. After these "meltdowns" children may fall asleep. Between these events, parents and caregivers often describe "walking on eggshells" in an attempt to avoid upsetting the child. When these behaviors are so severe that they significantly impair the child such that grades, social activities, and family participation are impaired, therapy and/or medications should be tried.

Initial evaluations will usually consist of a review of the child's basic health status, diet, medications, and major changes in the child's life. The behavioral history should be the focus. Bring with you any documentation from teachers or care providers to help further aid in the evaluation.

There are two classes of medications for this condition. Initially the "milder" class of alpha-adrenergic antagonists should be tried. These medications work by lowering the fight-or-flight chemicals that are thought to be too high. Most common side effects are dry mouth, tiredness, and dizziness. The more effective medications are second-generation neuroleptics, with risperidone (Risperdal) and aripiprazole (Abilify) being the two most common. Potential side effects include significant increase in appetite, weight gain, breast tissue tenderness/growth, and abnormal movements. Once starting this class of medications, parents can expect to see improvement in behavior within a few days. Because of the known metabolic side effects that occur in patients taking an atypical antipsychotic, baseline and periodic monitoring is recommended.

Developmental Disorders

Autism. Autism is a condition that affects approximately one out of forty boys and one out of two hundred girls. Parents usually first notice differences in their kids at around two years old. The three big areas where autistic children develop differently are in social interaction, communication, and restricted interests/repetitive behavior. People notice that these kids don't seem to seek out parents' approval. They may not like to cuddle or snuggle. Mothers in particular may feel the child doesn't love them due to the absence of the usual gazing between mothers and their babies. This lack of interest in social interaction affects autistic kids' interactions with other children. Autistic children may not have any interest in playing or even interacting at all with other children. They may be totally satisfied playing alone. Speech is usually delayed. Autistic toddlers may not say their first words for months to years after typical toddlers are speaking. These kids may repeat lines or phrases from a song or program over and over again. Autistic individuals can display many forms of repetitive or restricted behavior, such as hand flapping, head rolling, or body rocking.

There are also time-consuming behaviors intended to reduce anxiety that an individual feels compelled to perform repeatedly or according to rigid rules, such as placing objects in a specific order, checking things, or hand washing. There is also resistance to change—for example, insisting that the furniture not be moved or refusing to be interrupted—and an unvarying pattern of daily activities, such as an unchanging menu or a dressing ritual. In addition, there are interests or fixations that are abnormal in theme or intensity of focus, such as preoccupation with a single television program, toy, or game as well as such behaviors as eye poking, picking skin, hand biting, and head banging.

About half of parents of children with autism notice their children's unusual behaviors by age eighteen months, and four out of five notice by age twenty-four months.[10] According to an article, failure to meet any of the following milestones "is an absolute indication to proceed with further evaluations. Delay in referral for such testing may delay early diagnosis and treatment and affect the long-term outcome":[11]

- No <u>babbling</u> by twelve months
- No <u>gesturing</u> (pointing, waving, and so on) by twelve months
- No single words by sixteen months
- No two-word (spontaneous, not just <u>echolalia</u>) phrases by twenty-four months
- Any loss of any language or social skills at any age

There is no medication for autism per se. Medications can be used to help children be less irritable and aggressive or to decrease self-injurious behaviors. The more effective medications are second-generation neuroleptics, with risperidone and aripiprazole being the two most common. Potential side effects include significant increase in appetite, weight gain, breast tissue tenderness/growth, and abnormal movements. Once starting this class of medications, parents can expect to see improvement in behavior within a few days. Because of the known metabolic side effects that occur in patients taking an atypical antipsychotic, baseline and periodic monitoring is recommended.

Intellectual disabilities (mental retardation). An intellectual disability is an impairment in the child's mental abilities such that the child has more difficulty coping with everyday tasks. The intellect is affected, such as reading, writing, math, language, and memory. Social abilities are also affected, such as social/interpersonal skills and empathy. The practical domain is affected, such as money management, personal hygiene, and organizing and prioritizing work, school, and recreation.

Mostly this impairment is the diminished ability to effectively synthesize information and adapt to one's environment. Initial evaluations will usually consist of a review of the child's basic health status, diet, medications, and major changes in the child's life. The behavioral history should be the focus. Bring with you any documentation from teachers or care providers to help further aid in the evaluation.

There are no medications or therapies for this condition. One should focus on obtaining a comprehensive evaluation to ensure the correct diagnosis, securing the social security disability if qualified, enrolling the person in appropriate educational programs to pursue the person's maximum capacity, and promoting the most independent living possible.

Anxiety. Every child has experienced anxiety in one situation or another: prior to a performance, going to a new school, trying something new for the first time, and similar situations. Anxiety that persists beyond this and causes interference in regular activities could be an anxiety disorder. There are a few common types of anxiety in children.

Social anxiety—social phobia. These can be brought out by situations involving social interactions or performance where the child experiences excessive fear of being laughed at, ridiculed, embarrassed, or humiliated to the point that he or she avoids most if not all social interactions.

According to the National Institute of Mental Health (NIMH), social anxiety disorder symptoms include the following:

- Feeling highly anxious about being with other people and having a hard time talking to them
- Feeling very self-conscious in front of other people and worried about feeling humiliated, embarrassed, or rejected or being fearful of offending others
- Being very afraid that other people will judge them
- Worrying for days or weeks before an event where other people will be
- Staying away from places where there are other people
- Having a hard time making friends and keeping friends
- Blushing, sweating, or trembling around other people
- Feeling nauseous or sick to your stomach when other people are around

Panic disorder—panic attacks. A panic attack is the sudden onset of severe anxiety, worry, chest discomfort, feeling smothered, feeling trapped, sweating, shaking, and so on. This can lead to attempts to prevent another attack by avoiding the location where the attack occurred. This can lead to fewer and fewer places a person feels comfortable, until finally he or she rarely leaves the house (known as agoraphobia).

According to NIMH, panic disorder symptoms include the following:

- Sudden and repeated attacks of intense fear
- Feelings of being out of control during a panic attack
- Intense worries about when the next attack will happen
- Fear or avoidance of places where panic attacks have occurred in the past

Separation anxiety disorder. This is when a child is overcome with fear about separating or the idea of separating from his or her primary caretaker. Worry about death and dying is common. School refusal can lead to academic decline. They can feel and say that no one loves them or that no one cares about them. They can sometimes say they wish they were dead. They can be demanding or jealous or overprotective of their primary caretaker. This can put great strain on the parent/child relationship.

There are specific symptoms of separation anxiety disorder to watch for, including developmentally inappropriate and excessive anxiety concerning separation from home or from those to whom the individual is attached, as evidenced by three (or more) of the following:

- Recurrent excessive distress when separation from home or major attachment figures occurs or is anticipated
- Persistent and excessive worry about losing, or about possible harm befalling, major attachment figures
- Persistent and excessive worry that an untoward event will lead to separation from a major attachment figure (for example, getting lost or being kidnapped)
- Persistent reluctance or refusal to go to school or elsewhere because of fear of separation
- Persistently and excessively fearful or reluctant to be alone or without major attachment figures at home or without significant adults in other settings

- Persistent reluctance or refusal to go to sleep without being near a major attachment figure or to sleep away from home
- Repeated nightmares involving the theme of separation
- Repeated complaints of physical symptoms (such as headaches, stomachaches, nausea, or vomiting) when separation from major attachment figures occurs or is anticipated

The disturbance causes clinically significant distress or impairment in social, academic (occupational), or other important areas of functioning.[12]

Initial evaluations will usually consist of a review of the child's basic health status, diet, medications, and major changes in the child's life. The behavioral history should be the focus. Bring with you any documentation from teachers or care providers to help further aid in the evaluation.

The good news is that there are treatments for anxiety. Both individual and family therapy are recommended first. For example, cognitive behavioral therapy and interpersonal psychotherapy are forms of individual therapy shown to be effective in treating anxiety. Treatment may also include the use of antianxiety medication.

Notes

1. Ronald C. Kessler, Wai Tat Chiu, Olga Demler, and Ellen E. Walters, "Prevalence, Severity, and Comorbidity of 12-Month *DSM-IV* Disorders in the National Comorbidity Survey Replication," *Archives of General Psychiatry* 62, no. 6 (2005): 617–27.
2. Kathleen Ries Merikangas, Jian-Ping He, Debra Brody, Prudence W. Fisher, Karen Bourdon, and Doreen S. Koretz, "Prevalence and Treatment of Mental Disorders among US Children in the 2001–2004 NHANES," *Pediatrics* 125, no. 1 (2010): 75–81.
3. Carl C. Bell and Radhika Chimata, "Prevalence of Neurodevelopmental Disorders among Low-Income African Americans at a Clinic on Chicago's South Side," *Psychiatric Services* 66, no. 5 (2015): 539–42.

4. Rahn K. Bailey and Dion L. Owens, "Overcoming Challenges in the Diagnosis and Treatment of Attention-Deficit/Hyperactivity Disorder in African Americans," *Journal of the National Medical Association* 97, suppl. 10 (2005): 5S–10S.

5. The National Survey of Children's Exposure to Violence (NatSCEV) is the largest, most comprehensive survey on youth victimization incidence and prevalence conducted in the United States. NatSCEV is a joint effort funded by the US Department of Justice and the Centers for Disease Control and Prevention and is carried out by the University of New Hampshire's Crimes against Children Research Center.

6. Michelle V. Porche, Lisa R. Fortuna, Julia Y. Lin, and Margarita Alegria, "Childhood Trauma and Psychiatric Disorders as Correlates of School Dropout in a National Sample of Young Adults," *Child Development* 82, no. 3 (2011): 982–98.

7. Tania Das Banerjee, Frank Middleton, and Stephen V. Faraone, "Environmental Risk Factors for Attention-Deficit Hyperactivity Disorder," *Acta Pædiatrica* 96, no. 9 (2007): 1269–74.

8. Carl C. Bell, "Lessons Learned from 50 Years of Violence Prevention Activities in the African American Community," *Journal of the National Medical Association* 109, no. 4 (2017): 224–37.

9. "Depression in Children and Teens," American Academy of Child and Adolescent Psychiatry, accessed February 9, 2018, https://www.aacap.org/AACAP/Families_and_youth/Facts_for_Families/FFF-Guide/The-Depressed-Child-004.aspx.

10. Rebecca J. Landa, "Diagnosis of Autism Spectrum Disorders in the First 3 Years of Life," *Nature Clinical Practice Neurology* 4, no. 3 (2008): 138–47.

11. Pauline A. Filipek, Pasquale J. Accardo, Grace T. Baranek, Edwin H. Cook Jr., Geraldine Dawson, Barry Gordon, Judith S. Gravel, et al., "The Screening and Diagnosis of Autistic Spectrum Disorders," *Journal of Autism and Developmental Disorders* 29, no. 6 (1999): 439–84.

12. "Separation Anxiety Disorder Symptoms," Steve Bressert, *Psych Central*, accessed December 26, 2017, https://psychcentral.com/disorders/separation-anxiety-disorder-symptoms.

CHAPTER 9
Aging and Dementia

Don't We All Get a Little Forgetful?
MALAIKA E. BERKELEY, MD, MPH

What is dementia?

*D*ementia is a general term meaning a decline in memory, along with other difficulties in thinking that affects a person's ability to function in his or her personal and professional life.[1] Many people think that if you have dementia, you have Alzheimer's (mistakenly called "all timers" or "old timers" by some). In fact there are several types of dementia of which Alzheimer's is one.

Isn't some forgetfulness normal?

Some difficulty with memory is expected with age.[2] Normal decline in memory is minor compared to dementia. Age-related forgetfulness does not tend to get in the way of the person's independence and ability to perform basic tasks in the home. Normal aging also does not interfere with the ability to interact socially. Age-related memory decline also does not tend to lead to becoming disoriented or to having difficulties recognizing objects and close family. Here are some signs you may notice in the normal aging process:[3, 4]

- Decline in immediate memory (things learnt within the last few seconds)
- Occasional memory lapses
- Misplacing items occasionally
- Difficulty in word finding
- Taking longer to learn new things

How can I tell if my loved one has dementia?

A decline in memory is usually the first hint of dementia. This can be the only sign for years and tends to worsen over time. Other signs may come up later. The signs of dementia may be different depending on the type of dementia your loved one has. If you see any of these changes, you should seek an evaluation from a psychiatrist as soon as possible. The earlier you seek attention, the better your chances of slowing or stopping the decline. Some other signs of dementia include the following:[5]

- Difficulty communicating, recognizing objects, and finding words
- Difficulty following instructions and handling complex tasks
- Difficulty reasoning and problem solving
- Difficulty with planning and organizing
- Disorientation and confusion about people, dates, and one's location
- Difficulty with coordination and motor functions

Gladys is a sixty-eight-year-old grandmother and retired schoolteacher. Gladys's husband of fifty years passed away five years ago, but Gladys insisted on living alone in the same house where she had lived all her adult life and where she raised all four of her kids. About four years ago, she began to forget things like birthdays, which she had always known. She often confused or forgot the names of her grandkids and even those of her own kids. When Gladys began to lose such things as her keys, jewelry, and purse, she began to blame her family and visitors and started accusing them of stealing her things. The grandkids were beginning to tell Gladys's kids that when they stayed with Grandma for the weekend, she sometimes forgot the food on the stove and burned the pot. Gladys insisted that she didn't need help and refused to move in with any relatives. However, when a neighbor and good friend called Gladys's daughter to say she found Gladys wandering in the mall lost, the family decided to take her to the doctor.

What causes dementia?

Most dementias are age-related. Chances of developing dementia increase with age. Of people older than sixty-five, 15 percent have mild dementia and 5 percent have a severe dementia. Of those older than eighty, 20 percent have severe dementia.

The exact causes of dementia are still unclear but may be different based on the type of dementia. For many forms of dementia, it is believed that various types of proteins build up in the brain and damage the brain cells. This damage to brain cells seems to lead to a decline in the amount of nerve-related chemicals (neurotransmitters) that are thought to be involved in memory and thinking. Some of the more common types and causes of dementia include the following:

Alzheimer's dementia:

- This is the most common dementia. At least half of those with dementia have Alzheimer's.
- Genetic factors lead to proteins in the brain. Shrinkage of the brain is also noted.
- There is a greater chance of getting Alzheimer's dementia if you have an immediate family member with dementia.

Vascular dementia:

- This is the second most common type of dementia. It occurs in up to one-third of all dementias.

- The risk of vascular dementia is increased by conditions or habits that increase the risk of heart disease. These include smoking, obesity, hypertension and stroke, to name a few.
- Ten to fifteen percent of individuals have both vascular and Alzheimer's dementia.[6]

Substance-induced dementia:

- This is caused by damage to brain cells due to prolonged and extensive use of alcohol or illicit drugs.

HIV dementia:

- This is caused by infection with the HIV virus.

What should I expect at the psychiatrist's office?

It is essential that a family member attends all appointments because an informative history and progress report is necessary in diagnosing and monitoring dementia.[7] The psychiatrist will generally talk with you and your loved one together. He or she will typically take a full history of changes you have noticed lately, your loved one's previous ability to function, previous mental health care, physical health conditions, and medicines your loved one takes. You should come fully prepared with all this information to your first appointment with the psychiatrist. Having this information will increase the possibility that all other causes of memory problems are eliminated before a diagnosis of dementia is considered.

The psychiatrist may conduct a brief test of your loved one's functioning. Some of the more common tests include the Mini Mental Status Exam (MMSE)[8] and the Montreal Cognitive Assessment (MoCA).[9] The psychiatrist will usually order blood tests and sometimes a brain scan. He or she may recommend starting some medication while awaiting the results of further testing depending on the evaluation.

What is the purpose of further testing?

Although your loved one may appear to have signs of dementia, there are other conditions that have similar symptoms. Some of these conditions are treatable, and once treated, the dementia-like symptoms may improve or go away. These include thyroid disease, vitamin deficiencies, and even depression. It is helpful to get this testing in order to ensure that all possible conditions that may be affecting your loved one's health are addressed. Brain scans are less commonly done but can identify if there has been any injury to the brain, such as a stroke or brain tumor.[10]

Please keep in mind that most dementias cannot be diagnosed with certainty except by autopsy after your loved one has passed. This is not generally of significant concern as the treatment for most dementias is the same.

Gladys had begun to become slightly grumpier and more resistant over the last few years, so it was very difficult for her kids to convince her to go with them to the doctor. Through persistence and some trickery, her kids were eventually able to get her there. On the way there, Gladys did not seem to recognize many of the buildings and areas she grew up knowing and repeatedly referred to her daughter as her mother. The evaluation determined that Gladys was indeed suffering with dementia, most likely of the Alzheimer's type.

What treatment is available if my loved one has dementia?

If, after a full evaluation, your psychiatrist determines that your loved one has dementia, he or she will usually recommend some medication. These medications are generally aimed toward increasing the amount of certain chemicals (neurotransmitters) in the brain to help preserve memory and thinking.[11] The choice of medication is based on the severity of dementia (mild, moderate, or severe). Unfortunately, medications for dementia do not reverse the damage that has already occurred. However, it does tend to slow further decline in memory and function, allowing individuals to spend more quality time with loved ones. Sometimes other medications are recommended as well if there are any additional concerns, such as depression or aggression.

What should I expect (the prognosis) if my loved one has dementia?

At this time there is no cure for dementia. Current medications tend to slow the course of the dementia but cannot stop or reverse it. Most dementias tend to begin with very subtle signs of memory loss that progress gradually over a five- to ten-year time period. The affected individual's ability to maintain independence tends to lessen along with these changes.

Those affected gradually find difficulty in the ability to take care of finances and the household, which usually progresses into difficulty caring for their activities of daily living (ADL). ADLs include bathing, eating, dressing, and toileting oneself. As their ability to care for ADLs reduces, your loved one's need for caretaker supervision and assistance increases. Toward the moderate to severe stages of dementia, affected individuals tend to require twenty-four-hour supervision either at home or in a nursing home.

Some dementias, such as vascular dementias or those related to head trauma, can begin more suddenly. Such individuals may be able to maintain the same reduced level of functioning for some time, or they may follow a similar gradual course as mentioned earlier. However, a decline in ability to function on their own will generally occur.

Aside from medication, what else can I do for my loved one?

Because dementia tends to become more severe with time and lead to a decrease in your loved one's independence, it is generally necessary to provide additional help to the patient for his or her care, commonly called providing supervision. Initially this may be necessary for only a few hours a day and use of home health aides may prolong your loved one's ability to remain in his or her own home. For those who are still fairly independent, a senior living or assisted-living facility may be useful.[12]

As the dementia progresses, your loved one may require more supervision, eventually progressing to twenty-four-hour supervision. This may be accomplished by twenty-four-hour home health aides in the patient's home or in the home of a family member. If remaining in the home is not possible, then a memory care unit or a nursing home would be a suitable alternative.

Because those with declining memory can become easily confused about their surroundings, dates, and people, it is important to ensure that their days follow a routine. Day programs /adult day cares for the elderly can provide this needed routine and may also offer continued social contact.[13]

In order to keep confusion and chaos to a minimum, please encourage your loved one to choose a party or parties to take care of all legal and medical decisions. This should take the form of a legal document, such as a living will. This should be done early in the disease or, better yet, well before any significant illness appears.

Gladys was started on medication, which seemed to slow her memory loss. Gladys's family took over her finances and bills and did not allow Gladys to drive any more. Eventually, Gladys agreed to move in with her daughter and her family as she was in need of twenty-four-hour supervision. Gladys attended an adult day care three days a week. The family hired a home health aide for the days that Gladys did not go to the day care while her family supervised for her safety at night.

I feel guilty for asking, but what about me?

Life can become very hectic for those taking care of loved ones with dementia.[14] Most caretakers have their own personal and family responsibilities, which may now compete with caring for the individual with dementia. It can also be emotionally draining to watch the decline of a loved one.[15] In addition, those with dementia can also become aggressive and resistant to care. This can be very stressful for family members and may lead to some amount of guilt as difficult decisions may need to be made and restrictions imposed on previously independent loved ones. For this reason, it is generally a good idea for family members who are caretakers to engage in some stress-relieving activities of their own. Remember, you will be better able to take care of your loved one if you yourself are in good health mentally, physically, and spiritually. Some ideas include the following:

- Ask other family members to share in the responsibility and supervision.
- Enjoy and maintain your other relationships.
- Make sure that you are making time to do fun things for yourself.
- Consider taking your loved one to a respite home for a few days so that you may get some relief.
- Join a caretakers group so that you can have an outlet for your stress, get some ideas about coping with caretaking, and help relieve the guilt you may feel about difficult decisions.

Notes

1. "Evaluation of Cognitive Impairment and Dementia," Eric Larson, UpToDate, last updated September 20, 2017, https://www.uptodate.com/contents/evaluation-of-cognitive-impairment-and-dementia.
2. Ronald C. Petersen, G. E. Smith, Emre Kokmen, Robert J. Ivnik, and Eric G. Tangalos, "Memory Function in Normal Aging," *Neurology* 42, no. 2 (1992): 396.
3. Kaplan and Sadock, "Dementia."
4. Ibid.
5. Harrold Kaplan and Benjamin Sadock, "Dementia," in *Synopsis of Psychiatry*, by Benjamin Sadock and Harrold Kaplan (Baltimore: Lipincott, Williams & Wilkins, 1998), 328.
6. Ibid.
7. David B. Carr, Steven Gray, Jack Baty, and John C. Morris, "The Value of Informant versus Individual's Complaints of Memory Impairment in Early Dementia," *Neurology* 55, no. 11 (2000): 1724–26.

8. W. Freidl, R. Schmidt, W. J. Stronegger, A. Irmler, B. Reinhart, and M. Koch, "Mini Mental State Examination: Influence of Sociodemographic, Environmental and Behavioral Factors, and Vascular Risk Factors," *Journal of Clinical Epidemiology* 49, no. 1 (1996): 73–8.
9. Daniel H. J. Davis, Sam T. Creavin, Jennifer L. Y. Yip, Anna H. Noel-Storr, Carol Crayne, and Sarah Cullum, "Montreal Cognitive Assessment for the Diagnosis of Alzheimer's Disease and Other Dementias," *Cochrane Database of Systematic Reviews* (2015): CD010775.
10. Dale A. Charletta, Philip B. Gorelick, Timothy J. Dollear, Sally Freels, and Y. Harris, "CT and MRI Findings among African-Americans with Alzheimer's Disease, Vascular Dementia, and Stroke without Dementia," *Neurology* 45, no. 8 (1995): 1456–61.
11. Noll L. Campbell, Malaz Boustani, Kathleen A. Lane, S. Gao, Hugh Hendrie, Babar A. Khan, J. R. Murrell, et al., "Use of Anticholinergics and the Risk of Cognitive Impairment in an African American Population," *Neurology* 75, no. 2 (2010): 152–59.
12. Richard Schulz, Steven H. Belle, Sara J. Czaja, Kathleen A. McGinnis, Alan Stevens, and Song Zhang, "Long-Term Care Placement of Dementia Patients and Caregiver Health and Well-Being," *Journal of the American Medical Association* 292, no. 8 (2004): 961–67.
13. Maud J. L. Graff, Myrra J. M. Vernooij-Dassen, Marjolein Thijssen, Joost Dekker, Willibrord H. L. Hoefnagels, and Marcel G. M. OldeRikkert, "Effects of Community Occupational Therapy on Quality of Life, Mood, and Health Status in Dementia Patients and Their Caregivers: A Randomized Controlled Trial," *The Journals of Gerontology: Series A* 62, no. 9 (2007): 1002–09.
14. Philippe Thomas, Fabrice Lalloué, Pierre-Marie Preux, Cyril Hazif-Thomas, Sylvie Pariel, Robcis Inscale, Joël Belmin, and Jean-Pierre Clément, "Dementia Patients Caregivers Quality of Life: The PIXEL Study," *International Journal of Geriatric Psychiatry* 21, no. 1 (2006): 50–6.
15. Pim Cuijpers, "Depressive Disorders in Caregivers of Dementia Patients: A Systematic Review," *Aging & Mental Health* 9, no. 4 (2005): 325–30.

CHAPTER 10

Medication Management

Will the Medication Change Me?
KARRIEM L. SALAAM, MD

Sometimes medications are needed to treat mental health problems. It is important to remember that medications are only a part of the treatment plan, which might also include other types of treatment, such as talk therapy. The treatment plan should be made only after an evaluation has been completed and the need for using medication has been established. Most of the time, the doctor must get special permission from the patient, or the patient's parent or legal guardian if the patient is a minor, before prescribing medication. This special permission is called informed consent. Before prescribing medication, the doctor should explain (1) why the medication is being used, (2) how the medication could help, (3) what possible harm the medication could cause, (4) what other treatments are available other than the medication, and (5) the most common and most serious medication side effects. Psychiatric medications are used to treat target symptoms, such as sadness; worrying too much; problems like difficulty sitting still and paying attention; moodiness, anger, and fighting; strange thoughts and behaviors that do not make sense; or hearing voices that other people cannot hear. In this chapter we will talk about medications that are used to treat common mental health problems.

Tips When Taking Psychiatric Medications

Once the decision is made to take psychiatric medication, many people would like to know the following: (1) How long do I have to take the medication? (2) Do I have to take the medication for the rest of my life? The simplest answers to these questions depend on the target symptoms the medication is being used to treat and how severe these symptoms are. When starting psychiatric medications for the first time, I would recommend a trial period of two to three months. During and after the trial period, the doctor and patient are looking at how the target symptoms have responded to the medication, whether the dose of the medication should be changed, or if there are any side effects and what should be done about them. You should always ask your doctor about the medication he or she is prescribing for you or your relative and if he or she could provide you with reading material about the medication if he or she has not already done so. Some, although not all, psychiatric medications require a medical checkup, blood tests, or other medical tests, such as an electrocardiogram, or EKG, which looks at the electrical activity of the heart, to be completed to see how healthy the patient is before starting the medication. Finally, some, although not all, psychiatric medications, especially certain mood stabilizers, require that blood levels be checked to make sure that the right amount of medication is in the blood to be effective and that there is not too much to harm the body or to cause severe side effects.

Medicines Used to Treat Attention Deficit Hyperactivity Disorder

The medications that are most commonly used to treat attention deficit hyperactivity disorder (ADHD) are called stimulants. The most well-known stimulant is methylphenidate (Ritalin); other commonly used stimulants include mixed amphetamine salts (Adderall), and lisdexamphetamine (Vyvanse). Stimulant medications can be long-acting, where you need to take them only once a day in the morning, or short-acting, where you might have to take them two or three times a day. Stimulants are used to treat the target symptoms of ADHD, such as not being able to sit still, not being able to focus and concentrate, and talking and acting without thinking first. It is important to remember that ADHD used to be called ADD (attention deficit disorder), so when people talk about ADD and ADHD, they are talking about the same disorder. It is also important to remember that some people who have ADHD are not hyperactive; they only have problems focusing, concentrating, and remembering things. ADHD is one of the most common reasons children are seen by psychiatrists.

Stimulant medications work by helping brain cells communicate more effectively. Brain cells make several chemicals called neurotransmitters, which they use to communicate with one another. Dopamine and norepinephrine are the two neurotransmitters that stimulant medications affect to help brain cells communicate better.[1] Some things you might notice if the medication is working well include improved ability to sit still, focus, and concentrate and fewer complaints about the child's behavior from teachers, coaches, babysitters, Sunday school teachers, and other adults who are involved in the child's life. With stimulant medication and other supports as part of a complete treatment plan, the child's behavior, grades in school, and ability to participate in activities with other children should improve.

Like any medications, stimulant medications have side effects. In this section we will talk about some of the most common and more serious side effects. If after taking the medication, your mouth, throat, or skin starts itching or you get a rash or hives (bumpy red rash in spots or patches on the skin), you have swelling of the lips and tongue, or you feel like your throat is closing and you cannot breathe, *stop* the medication and get medical care immediately. These are symptoms of an allergic reaction, and if you are allergic to a medication, you should *not* take that medication again.[2]

Common side effects of stimulant medications used to treat ADHD include the following:

- Low appetite and weight loss, so the medication should be given with or right after meals.

- Problems falling asleep, so lowering the dose or changing the time the medication is given could help with this.
- Increased heart rate (heart racing) and blood pressure, which is why the doctor should check the child's heart rate (pulse) and blood pressure while the child is taking stimulant medication.

Less common but more serious side effects include the following:

- Stuttering and tics (quick, repeated movements or sounds, such as nodding the head to one side or clearing the throat).
- Slower growth, so the doctor should check the child's height and weight while he or she is taking the medicine. Growth usually improves if the medication is stopped or the dose is lowered.
- Seeing, hearing, or feeling things that others cannot see, hear, or feel, such as feeling like bugs are crawling on the skin or hearing voices.

Medicines Used to Treat Anxiety

Two major groups of medications are used to treat anxiety: benzodiazepines (benzos for short) and selective serotonin reuptake inhibitors. Other medications, such as buspirone (Buspar), are also used to treat anxiety; however, they do not belong to a major group of medications. Because selective serotonin reuptake inhibitors are more commonly used to treat depression, they will be discussed in the next section on medications used to treat depression. Some of the better-known benzos are alprazolam (Xanax), clonazepam (Klonopin), lorazepam (Ativan), and diazepam (Valium). Benzos can be long-acting, where you take them once or twice a day in the morning and evening, or shorter-acting, where you might take them only when you need them to stop anxiety before it starts or to stop or lower the anxiety once it has already started. Benzos are used to treat the target symptoms of anxiety, such as worrying too much, feeling too nervous, or feeling too afraid to the point where you cannot function at home, at work, or in school. Benzos have been helpful for people with generalized anxiety disorder, panic disorder, posttraumatic stress disorder, and social phobia.

Benzos work by affecting a neurotransmitter called GABA to help brain cells communicate more effectively and soothe parts of the brain that are too activated in people who are anxious.[3] Some things you might notice if the medication is working well include less worrying, fewer symptoms of anxiety attacks (heart racing, shortness of breath, lightheadedness, and sweating), and fewer specific fears, called phobias, such as fear of heights, fear of flying, or fear of the dark. Benzos can lower anxiety symptoms enough so that patients can learn specific therapies, including exposure therapy or cognitive behavioral therapy, to help them manage their anxiety symptoms. Sometimes with enough practice using these specific therapies, patients can learn to manage their symptoms with less medication or no medication at all.

Like any medications, medications used to treat anxiety have side effects. In this section we will talk about some of the most common and more serious side effects. If after taking the medication, your mouth, throat, or skin starts itching or you get a rash or hives (bumpy red rash in spots or patches on the skin), you have swelling of the lips and tongue, or you feel like your throat is closing and you cannot breathe, *stop* the medication and get medical care immediately. These are symptoms of an allergic reaction, and if you are allergic to a medication, you should *not* take that medication again.

Common side effects of medications used to treat anxiety include the following:

- Daytime drowsiness
- Clumsiness and coordination problems
- Poor memory and concentration

Less common but more serious side effects include the following:

- Addiction, since benzos affect the same part of the brain affected by alcohol

- Loss of consciousness and ability to breathe; therefore, benzos should *never* be used with alcohol
- Severe, out-of-control behavior, also called disinhibition

Red alerts:

- Some people use benzos to get high, so you must keep them out of reach of children and people who use drugs and alcohol.
- Benzo withdrawal could be dangerous and life-threatening; therefore, the dose of benzos must be lowered slowly and not stopped quickly.

Buspirone is a short-acting anxiety medication, so it has to be taken three times a day. Buspirone does not get rid of symptoms quickly like benzos; however, some doctors prefer buspirone because it is not addictive, and there is no risk of withdrawal, so it could be stopped immediately. Side effects include lightheadedness, restlessness, and sleep problems.

Medicines Used to Treat Depression

There are five major groups of medications used to treat depression: SSRIs (selective serotonin reuptake inhibitors), SNRIs (serotonin-norepinephrine reuptake inhibitors), TCAs (tricyclic antidepressants), MAOIs (monoamine oxidase inhibitors), and atypical antidepressants. TCAs and MAOIs are not usually the first, second, or third choice of medication used to treat depression; therefore, they are more important when talking about the history of antidepressant medications. It is more important to review the SSRIs, SNRIs, and atypical antidepressants, which are more likely to be prescribed by a psychiatrist or primary care physician. Some of the better-known SSRIs are fluoxetine (Prozac), sertraline (Zoloft), and paroxetine (Paxil). The best-known SNRIs are venlafaxine (Effexor), duloxetine (Cymbalta), and desvenlafaxine (Pristiq). The best-known atypical antidepressants include buproprion (Wellbutrin), mirtazapine (Remeron), and trazodone (Desyrel). Antidepressants, like other psychiatric medications, can be long-acting, where you take them once a day, or shorter-acting, where you take them two or three times a day. Antidepressants are used to treat the target symptoms of depression, such as sad or irritable mood; loss of interest or pleasure in what you used to enjoy; changes in sleep, energy, appetite, and concentration; feelings of guilt; and thoughts of dying or ending your life. SSRIs and SNRIs have been helpful for people with depression, anxiety symptoms, posttraumatic stress disorder (PTSD), and obsessive-compulsive disorder (OCD).

SSRIs work by increasing the neurotransmitter serotonin, whose activity has been low in specific areas of the brain in some people with depression and anxiety.[4] SNRIs work like SSRIs; however, they increase two neurotransmitters, serotonin and norepinephrine, in specific areas of the brain to treat symptoms of depression and anxiety.[5] It is important to remember that medications used to treat depression do not work immediately; some take two weeks to start working, on average four to six weeks to work well, and sometimes from eight to twelve weeks to work their best. Some things you might notice if the medication is working well include your mood slowly getting better, more energy, fewer sleep problems, more enjoyment in life (especially things you used to enjoy), fewer feelings of hopelessness and guilt, and a greater desire to live than to die. Antidepressant medications are not "happy pills," but they can lower depression enough so that the patient can learn specific therapies, including cognitive behavioral therapy (CBT) or interpersonal psychotherapy (IPT), to help manage the symptoms of depression.

Like any medications, medications used to treat depression have side effects. In this section we will talk about some of the most common and more serious side effects. If after taking the medication, your mouth, throat, or skin starts itching or you get a rash or hives (bumpy red rash in spots or patches on the skin), you have swelling of the lips and tongue, or you feel like your throat is closing and you cannot breathe, *stop* the medication and get medical care immediately. These are symptoms of an allergic reaction, and if you are allergic to a medication, you should *not* take that medication again.

Common side effects of medications used to treat depression include the following:

- Stomach upset, nausea, vomiting, or diarrhea
- Nervousness, restlessness, shakiness, and dizziness
- Dry mouth
- Loss of interest in sex, poor sexual performance

Less common but more serious side effects include the following:

- Thoughts of ending your life or trying to hurt yourself
- Increased energy, racing thoughts, increased mood swings, and sleeplessness could mean mania brought on by using an antidepressant in someone with bipolar disorder.

Red alerts:

- Muscle stiffness, shaking, high fever, jerking of the muscles, confusion, and red flushing of the skin could mean serotonin syndrome, which could be very dangerous and possibly life-threatening. Stop the medication immediately and seek urgent medical care.[6]

TCAs can be taken once or more than once a day, and they work like SNRIs by increasing serotonin and norepinephrine in specific areas of the brain to treat depression, anxiety, and OCD symptoms.[7] Fewer side effects occur if the TCA is started at a low dose and increased slowly. Side effects include dry mouth, constipation, dizziness, blurry vision, daytime drowsiness, and difficulty urinating.
Red alerts:

- Seizures
- Racing heart
- Confusion (seek urgent medical care)

- TCAs should not be used with alcohol or benzos because of increased risk of drowsiness and loss of consciousness.
- TCA overdoses can be quite dangerous due to abnormal electrical activity in the heart.

MAOIs were the first medications developed to treat depression. They work by increasing the neurotransmitters serotonin, norepinephrine, and dopamine in certain areas of the brain involved in depression. Side effects include dry mouth, drowsiness, lightheadedness, nausea, diarrhea and constipation, low interest in sex, jerking of muscles, and difficulty urinating.[8]

Red alerts:

- MAOIs should not be used within one month of using a TCA, an SSRI, an SNRI, or an atypical antidepressant as this could lead to dangerously high blood pressure.
- MAOIs should not be used with foods liked cured and smoked meats, such as pepperoni, hot dogs, and anchovies, certain wines like chianti, and smoked and aged cheeses that contain large amounts of tyramine as this could also lead to dangerously high blood pressure. Because you have to be so careful with your diet while taking MAOIs, they are not a good choice for people who have problems with binge eating.
- MAOIs should not be used with certain cold and allergy medications because this could lead to dangerous drug interactions.[9]

Atypical antidepressants like bupropion SR and XL, mirtazapine, and trazodone are called atypical because they do not fit neatly into any other larger group of antidepressant medications. Because they are longer-acting, atypical antidepressants are usually taken no more than twice a day. Immediate-release bupropion is short-acting, so it can be taken up to three times a day. Bupropion is an antidepressant that can be used for behavior problems in children with ADHD. Under the brand name Zyban, bupropion has also been used to help people who are trying to quit smoking. Bupropion works by increasing the neurotransmitters dopamine and norepinephrine to help brain cells communicate with one another more effectively.[10] Mirtazapine can increase appetite and cause drowsiness, so it might be helpful for someone whose depression has caused problems with sleep, appetite, and weight loss. Mirtazapine is usually given at bedtime. Trazodone can be used to treat depression, nervousness, aggression, and irritable mood; however, it is most commonly used to help people fall asleep. Mirtazapine and trazodone are often used as nighttime sleep medications even for those who may not have problems with depression or anxiety. They are usually given at bedtime. Trazodone works by increasing the neurotransmitter serotonin in certain areas of the brain.[11]

Side effects include the following:

- **Bupropion:** anxiety, restlessness, crankiness, dry mouth, problems sleeping
- **Mirtazapine:** sleepiness, constipation, dry mouth, increased appetite, weight gain
- **Trazodone:** daytime sleepiness, blurry vision, frequent erections in males

Red alerts:

- **Bupropion:** Seizures are more likely if you take more than 400 mg/day, you are drinking alcohol, or you have frequent vomiting.[12] Bupropion should not be used if you have a seizure disorder (epilepsy) or an eating disorder where you make yourself vomit.
- **Mirtazapine:** Muscle stiffness, shaking, high fever, jerking of the muscles, confusion, and red flushing of the skin could mean serotonin syndrome, which could be very dangerous and possibly life-threatening. Stop the medication immediately and seek urgent medical care.[13]

- **Trazodone:** In males, a strong but painful erection for more than an hour (called priapism) could lead to impotence (erectile dysfunction).[14] Consider not using trazodone for males; many men, when told of this rare side effect, choose to use a different medication for sleep. Trazodone can also cause serotonin syndrome.

Black Box Warning
In 2004, the Food and Drug Administration (FDA) told drug companies to add a black box warning to all antidepressants when prescribed to youths. Some minors have more suicidal thoughts and behaviors (such as cutting themselves) when they are started on an antidepressant medication. In the research studies of more than four thousand minors that led to the black box warning, antidepressant medications did not lead to *any* minors taking their own lives. It is important to remember that untreated depression has been the cause of many people taking their own lives. The doctor (or other prescriber) of the antidepressant must talk about the black box warning with the patient and/or his or her parent or legal guardian. These suicidal thoughts and behaviors are more likely to happen in the first few weeks to months of treatment. During this time, the prescriber should monitor the patient closely so that the prescriber can help the patient in case suicidal thoughts and behaviors develop or worsen.[15]

Medicines Used to Treat Aggression or Changes in Mood
The medicines used to treat aggression and changes in mood are called mood stabilizers. Mood stabilizers include lithium (Eskalith/Lithobid); the anticonvulsant medications (commonly used to treat seizures), such as valproic acid (Depakote), carbamazepine (Tegretol), oxcarbazepine (Trileptal), and lamotrigine (Lamictal); and atypical antipsychotics, such as aripiprazole (Abilify), risperidone (Risperdal), olanzapine (Zyprexa), ziprasidone (Geodon), and clozapine (Clozaril). Of the atypical antipsychotics, only aripiprazole will be discussed in this section; the other antipsychotics will be discussed in the

next section on medications used to treat disorganized thoughts, behaviors, and voices. Mood stabilizers, like other psychiatric medications, can be taken once a day or more than once a day depending on if they are long-acting or short-acting. Mood stabilizers are used to treat the following target symptoms: anger, aggression, property damage, mood swings, and mania (which are common in bipolar disorder). Atypical antipsychotics can also be used to treat disruptive behaviors in minors, people who have had head injuries, and minors with autism spectrum disorders and intellectual disabilities (mental retardation). Some mood stabilizers, such as lithium and aripiprazole, can help antidepressants work better. Lithium works by stabilizing brain cells (neurons); the anticonvulsant mood stabilizers work by stabilizing part of the brain cells and by changing the amount of the specific brain chemicals (neurotransmitters) GABA and/or glutamate.[16] The atypical antipsychotics work by lowering the effect of two neurotransmitters, dopamine and serotonin, in specific parts of the brain.[17] Lithium and certain anticonvulsant mood stabilizers require blood (serum) levels to be checked to make sure that the correct amount of medication is in the bloodstream.

Like any medications, mood stabilizers have side effects. In this section we will talk about some of the most common and more serious side effects. If after taking the medication, your mouth, throat, or skin starts itching or you get a rash or hives (bumpy red rash in spots or patches on the skin), you have swelling of the lips and tongue, or you feel like your throat is closing and you cannot breathe, *stop* the medication and get medical care immediately. These are symptoms of an allergic reaction, and if you are allergic to a medication, you should *not* take that medication again.

Side effects include the following:

- **Lithium:** weight gain, diarrhea, shaky hands, thirstiness, frequent urination, acne, rash. Lithium could cause lower thyroid function, leading the patient to complain of always feeling tired with slowed thinking and changes in hair, where the hair begins to feel rough. Too much lithium (lithium toxicity) could lead to difficulty walking or standing, worse shaking, and confusion.[18]

- **Anticonvulsants:** daytime drowsiness, stomach discomfort, walking unsteadily, poor coordination
- **Atypical antipsychotics:** daytime drowsiness, increase in appetite and weight, constant restlessness, slow movement and inability to change the look on your face, muscle stiffness (of the neck, jaw, or tongue)
- **Mood stabilizers** could interact with other medications or food, which could lead to more side effects or to the medication not working the way it should.

Red alerts:

- **Lithium:** Severe lithium toxicity could lead to seizures, abnormal heartbeat, and loss of consciousness. Lithium overdose could be dangerous and life threatening.[19]
- **Anticonvulsants:** Side effects that require immediate medical attention are dark urine, light-colored feces, yellow skin or eyes, bleeding and easy bruising, sore throat, fever, vomiting, and rash.[20]
- **Atypical antipsychotics:** Thirstiness, frequent urination, low energy, and blurred vision could be diabetes. High fever, muscle stiffness and confusion, or trouble breathing and/or swallowing are medical emergencies.[21]

Medicines Used to Treat Disorganized Thoughts, Behaviors, and Voices

The medicines used to treat disorganized thoughts, behaviors, and voices are called antipsychotics. The newer antipsychotics are called atypical or second-generation antipsychotics; the older antipsychotics, which are no longer commonly used outside of the hospital, are called typical or first-generation antipsychotics. The atypical antipsychotics include risperidone (Risperdal), olanzapine (Zyprexa), ziprasidone (Geodon), and clozapine (Clozaril). The typical antipsychotics include chlorpromazine

(Thorazine) and haloperidol (Haldol). Antipsychotics, like other medications, can be taken once a day or more than once a day depending on if they are long-acting or short-acting. Antipsychotic medications are used to treat the following target symptoms: hearing voices and seeing things that other people cannot hear or see (hallucinations) and false beliefs where there is no proof for these beliefs, such as aliens from Mars using chips they implanted in the brains of all humans to get them pregnant so that these children could kidnap the sun. These false beliefs are called delusions. Other target symptoms include speech, thoughts, and behaviors that do not make sense. The newer or atypical antipsychotics also treat target symptoms, such as low energy and motivation to do anything and staying away from others (social isolation).

All these symptoms together are called symptoms of psychosis that could be seen in such disorders as schizophrenia, mania (bipolar disorder or manic depression), and really bad depression. Atypical antipsychotics can also be used to treat mood swings, agitation, aggression, and serious behavior problems in minors with disruptive behavior disorders (conduct disorder and oppositional defiant disorder), intellectual disabilities (mental retardation), autism spectrum disorders (autism, Asperger's, and pervasive development disorder), and people who have had head injuries. The atypical antipsychotics work by lowering the effect of two neurotransmitters, dopamine and serotonin, in specific parts of the brain. The older, typical, or first-generation antipsychotics work by lowering the effect of the neurotransmitter (brain chemical) dopamine in specific areas of the brain. Sometimes lowering the effect of dopamine in other parts of the brain can lead to medication side effects.[22]

Like any medications, antipsychotics have side effects. In this section we will talk about some of the most common and more serious side effects. If after taking the medication, your mouth, throat, or skin starts itching or you get a rash or hives (bumpy red rash in spots or patches on the skin), you have swelling of the lips and tongue, or you feel like your throat is closing and you cannot breathe, *stop* the medication and get medical care immediately.

These are symptoms of an allergic reaction, and if you are allergic to a medication, you should *not* take that medication again.

Side effects include the following:

- Daytime drowsiness, increased appetite and weight gain, dry mouth, constipation, and blurry vision; increased restlessness and powerful urge to keep moving and not stay still; slower movement and inability to change the look on your face; muscle stiffness (of the neck, jaw, or tongue); low motivation for sex

Red alerts:

- Seizures, overheating, thirstiness, frequent urination, low energy, and blurred vision could be diabetes. High fever, muscle stiffness and confusion, or severe trouble breathing and/or swallowing are all medical emergencies. *Call 911 or go to the emergency room ASAP.*[23]
- A rare side effect of antipsychotic medication that could be permanent is called tardive dyskinesia (TD). TD is repeated movements of the face, lips, tongue, arms, legs, or body that the person cannot control or stop. Someone could develop TD after being on antipsychotic medication for many months or years. If you notice movements that are not normal that started after you had been on the medication for a while, you can talk to the psychiatrist about changing to a medication that is less likely to cause TD. Sometimes if you stop or switch the medication quickly enough, the TD could go away.[24] It is very important to tell the doctor about any medication side effects.

Clozapine is a powerful medication used to treat disorganized thoughts, behaviors, and voices when other atypical antipsychotics have not been able to help with these problems. Clozapine could take a long time (weeks to months) before it starts working. It can also help with such symptoms as low energy and motivation to get anything done and staying away from other people (social isolation). Clozapine, like the other atypical antipsychotics, also works by lowering the effect of two neurotransmitters, dopamine and serotonin, in specific parts of the brain. Unlike the other atypical antipsychotics, clozapine has a very serious side effect, which is why you use clozapine only if the other atypical antipsychotics have been tried and shown not to work. Clozapine can cause a severe drop in the number of blood cells, which could lead to bleeding problems and serious infections. While taking clozapine, a special lab test (blood test) to check the number of specific white cells in the blood (neutrophils) must be done every week. The pharmacy is only allowed to give you the clozapine if you have enough neutrophils in your blood.[25] Because of this serious side effect, clozapine should only be given to people who are able to get the blood test done every week. There have been cases where clozapine has helped people with severe psychotic symptoms get rid of or lower their symptoms to where they could function. It is very important to know the serious side effect of using clozapine.

Common Questions about Psychiatric Medications

Will the medication make me look like a zombie?
The goal of psychiatric medication is not to make a person look like a zombie. Some of these medications might cause drowsiness, especially when you first start them or when you increase the dose. The concern of being made to look like a zombie comes up a lot when the discussion involves starting a child on medication, especially ADHD medications. One side effect of ADHD medication is that it can cause someone to stare into space. When parents of a child with ADHD ask about this, I encourage them to focus on things they can count, such as how many times they are getting calls from the school. Number of school suspensions? Number of trips to the principal's office? Number of poor or failing grades in school due to lost or missed schoolwork? Rates of school failure? Rates of juvenile delinquency? Number of high-risk behaviors, such as experimenting with cigarettes, alcohol, and drugs? Early experimentation with sex and its negative consequences, such as unplanned

pregnancy or sexually transmitted diseases? The medications used to treat ADHD decrease all these risks. It is difficult to describe how the medication makes you look like a zombie and even more difficult to measure how much of a zombie it makes you look like.

Will I get addicted to the medication?
Some psychiatric medications have a higher risk of addiction than others. Most psychiatric medications have no risk of addiction. The psychiatric medications that have the highest risk of addiction are benzodiazepines, such as clonazepam, alprazolam, and diazepam, which are used to treat anxiety symptoms, and stimulant medications, such as Adderall (mixed amphetamine salts), that are used to treat ADHD. To lower the risk of abuse of these medications, the Drug Enforcement Administration (DEA) monitors these medications very closely, including the doctors who prescribe them and the drugstores that dispense them. It is important that these medications are kept away from unsupervised children and teenagers and those who have a history of addiction or a strong family history of addiction. Untreated psychiatric disorders, like such mood disorders as depression and bipolar disorder, anxiety disorders, and PTSD, are all associated with high risks of substance use problems that could outweigh the risks of addiction caused by these medications.

Will I have to be on this medication for the rest of my life?
The simplest answer to this question depends on the target symptoms the medication is being used to treat and how severe these symptoms are. When starting psychiatric medications for the first time, I would recommend a trial period of two to three months. During and after the trial period, the doctor and patient are looking at how the target symptoms have responded to the medication, whether the dose of the medication should be changed, or if there are any side effects and what should be done about them. If the decision is made to stop the medication, this should be done only under a doctor's supervision, and you should be taken off the medication slowly. This is called a medication taper. During the medication taper, if the target symptoms return, the patient and the doctor have to make a decision about whether to continue the medication trial.

Why do I need this medication? That's only for "crazy people," and I'm not crazy.

Psychiatric medications are not for "crazy people"; they are for people who have problems with their brains that make it difficult for them to function at their best, no different from the way insulin is used to help people manage their blood sugar control so that they also can function at their best. The difference is the stigma or negative feelings many people have toward psychiatric diagnoses and treatment that many do not have toward such physical illnesses as diabetes, breast cancer, and heart disease. Psychiatric medications are a treatment tool to help those who are suffering from disorders of the mind and brain function at their best.

What would happen if you take the medication and you're getting high?

It is very important for the doctor who is prescribing the psychiatric medication for you to know about all the medications, nutritional supplements, and recreational substances, including illegal drugs, that are being taken along with the psychiatric medications. There is always the risk of negative interactions, also known as drug-drug interactions, when recreational drugs or alcohol is used at the same time as psychiatric medications. It is probably good common sense and clinical sense to tell the patients to stop using illegal drugs while they are taking psychiatric medications.

Will the medication mess up my system if I take it with my other medications?

Any specific damage caused by the medication depends on the specific medication being used. The more medications you are taking, the greater the chance there is for a drug-drug interaction. There are computer programs that allow you to enter the names of your medications and then see if there are any serious drug-drug interactions to be aware of.

What do I do if I want to get off the medication?

Talk to your psychiatrist (or other prescriber) about how you could be tapered off the medication slowly while watching carefully for medication side effects that occur as you are lowering the dose of the medication. You should also watch for the return of target symptoms of the psychiatric disorder while the medication dose is being lowered.

Who is going to check for medication side effects? How?
The psychiatrist (or other prescriber) who is prescribing the psychiatric medication should check for medication side effects. This is done by asking the patient general and specific questions about medication side effects. The psychiatrist should ask about the most common and the most serious medication side effects. There are also specific clinical tools that psychiatrists use to evaluate patients for specific groups of medication side effects, such as the Abnormal Involuntary Movement Scale (AIMS) that is used to check for movement-related side effects of antipsychotic medications.

Medications are one of many tools used by the psychiatrist to treat mental health conditions. Psychiatric medications should be prescribed only to treat specific target symptoms. The prescriber should monitor the patient closely to determine how well the medication(s) are working and for side effects the patient might be experiencing. Medication treatment should be done in collaboration with the patient and his or her primary care physician to increase the likelihood of a positive outcome while decreasing the risk of such serious medical issues as drug-drug interactions. Whenever possible before prescribing psychiatric medication, the benefit of medication use should outweigh the risk of serious medication side effects. When used appropriately psychiatric medications can reduce the burden of mental health problems while helping patients function at their best.

Notes

1. Mina K. Dulcan, *Helping Parents, Youth, and Teachers Understand Medications for Behavioral and Emotional Problems: A Resource Book of Medication Information Handouts*, 3rd ed. (Washington, DC: American Psychiatric Association, 2007), 13.
2. Ibid., 14–5.
3. Ibid., 3.

4. Ibid., 115.
5. Ibid., 683.
6. "Serotonin Syndrome," MedlinePlus Medical Encyclopedia, last updated December 21, 2017, https://medlineplus.gov/ency/article/007272.htm.
7. Mina K. Dulcan, *Helping Parents, Youth, and Teachers Understand Medications for Behavioral and Emotional Problems*, 127–28, 467.
8. Benjamin J. Sadock, Virginia A. Sadock, and Pedro Ruiz, *Kaplan & Sadock's Synopsis of Psychiatry: Behavioral Sciences/Clinical Psychiatry*, 11th ed. (Philadelphia: Wolters Kluwer, 2015), 994–95.
9. Ibid., 995–96.
10. Mina K. Dulcan, *Helping Parents, Youth, and Teachers Understand Medications for Behavioral and Emotional Problems*, 69.
11. Ibid., 637.
12. Ibid., 70.
13. Ibid., 446–47.
14. Ibid., 638.
15. Ibid., 276.
16. Ibid., 388, 671.
17. Ibid., 25.
18. Ibid., 390.
19. Ibid., 391.
20. Ibid., 673.
21. Ibid., 27.
22. Ibid., 341.
23. Ibid., 343.
24. Ibid., 343.
25. Ibid., 166.

CHAPTER 11

Treatment Options Other Than Medication

Do I Have to Take Pills?
ERICKA L. GOODWIN, MD

A lot of people have heard of psychiatry but may not fully understand the scope of what psychiatry really is. The media often portray people taking pills or sitting on an aloof person's couch. It is not rare to see characters in movies or television talking about taking their Xanax, Valium, or Prozac. Psychiatry is much more than that. It's treatment of the mind and spirit, so a wide variety of tools come in handy to help people. The science of psychiatry is the ability to correctly diagnose mental illnesses. The art of psychiatry is the ability to understand each person as a unique human being and to address him or her with a personalized strategy to restore health and to allow the person to be his or her best self. This chapter will explore a variety of these additional tools.

Gloria is a forty-two-year-old African American woman who loves children and is a teacher. She has two children of her own and a loving husband. She had been experiencing some sadness and difficulty sleeping, along with less of an appetite. She had still been able to work and take care of her responsibilities at home. She has always been a hard worker and a caretaker. She was the oldest of four children and often took care of her younger siblings. She was used to putting on a smile and not complaining. She didn't feel that she could afford to not get things done. In fact most people didn't even notice that anything was wrong. She felt even more alone because she felt like no one understood or recognized her suffering. She decided to see a therapist because she felt tired of feeling like she was living life in a fog. She's attended only two sessions so far but is interested in whether there are treatment options other than medication to get her back to feeling like her old self.

If I am diagnosed with a mental illness, do I have to take medication?

First, a diagnosis is a description, not an identity. Remember that you are not your illness. Regarding whether one needs medication, it depends on the severity and the condition. There are a variety of nonmedication treatments available for mental health conditions. These treatments can be used on their own or to complement medication interventions. There are times when the severity and impairment from a mental health issue are so severe that medication cannot be avoided. Consequently, during treatment, the need for medication is continuously being evaluated and adjustments are made to make sure that each person receives the best treatment possible, receives treatment that is personally tailored to him or her, and receives the best chance of success, including moving past a mental health issue.

Why would one use treatments other than medication?

Sometimes medication is not needed because the condition is not severe enough or the risks of medication (side effects) outweigh the potential benefits. Additional treatments may be needed to combat side effects from medication, including weight gain or insomnia. Other options can be used to further enhance treatment with medication.

If the condition is not severe enough to need medication, why would one need any treatment?

Everyone deserves to be their best selves. Just because someone is getting by doesn't mean that is as good as it gets. Every person deserves to live a life that is full of love, happiness, and productivity. Mental health issues can take away from different areas of our lives and can also significantly affect relationships. Getting things done at home and work can be affected by poor concentration. Irritability and withdrawn behavior can all affect relationships, even at work. Feeling stressed affects the body, including releasing stress hormones like cortisol, which encourage the body to gain weight. Gaining weight is a frustration and stressor on its own. It doesn't make sense for anyone to suffer just because he or she perceives the suffering to not be severe.

What are some treatments used that are not medications?

One of the most commonly used nonmedication interventions is psychotherapy, also known as talk therapy. There are also nutritional interventions, meditation, yoga, sleep hygiene, and exercise. One of the beautiful things about a lot of these interventions is that they have usefulness outside of the immediate treatment of a mental health issue and can be used to improve overall health even after someone feels better.

Can I pray mental health issues away?

Prayer is a powerful tool and can be an integral part of the mind-body-spirit connection. Feeling connected to a greater power or to the universe is a strength and source of healing power. Prayer has been shown to have a positive influence on mental health.[1] Plus there is a sense of peace that can be gained from prayer. Unfortunately, there are times when prayer is not enough to get someone feeling back to health. Think of it like getting a big cut; you can pray that it gets better, but it still needs some ointment and time to heal. Prayer may not always be able to right the biochemical disturbances on its own. This is one of the reasons pastoral counselors and counselors in the church are often taught about situations that are serious enough that additional medical attention is needed. Even if additional help is needed, prayer still remains a great resource and source of inspiration. Spirituality often provides a framework for a greater purpose for life, which helps people feel that there is a reason they exist. This sense of purpose allows people to think about themselves in the future and consequently visualize themselves in the future. This helps them to have inspiration to keep moving forward in more difficult times and experiences.

I hear people talk about therapy. Is there just one type of therapy?

There are multiple types of psychotherapy or talk therapy. Therapy is more than what is classically shown on TV and in movies. Also, the myths that therapy is for people with money or for folks without real problems are false. Types of psychotherapy range from supportive (where someone listens to you talk and provides nuggets of assistance along the way) to more structured therapy, such as cognitive behavioral therapy, or CBT (a therapy that looks at thoughts, perceptions, and behaviors and offers specific intervention to change thoughts and behaviors that are causing problems). Other therapies include interpersonal, exposure, psychodynamic, and analysis. The important takeaway is that there are many therapies to fit a variety of situations and communication styles. One of the critical elements of therapy is the ability to be open, honest, and vulnerable with a therapist, so it is very important to identify a therapist who you feel comfortable with. It's like finding a mate; you need the right fit. If one therapist or type of therapy does not work, it does not mean that therapy cannot be effective for you.

Why do some people shy away from the idea of going to therapy?

There have been some myths that therapy is only for white people. Also, some people are concerned that information discussed in therapy will be used against them, including affecting their jobs or causing them to lose their children. This includes fear of the paper trail left by insurance. There has also been some historical mistrust in medicine that may transfer over to the therapy, especially because a core part of therapy is being vulnerable. Experimentation on or mistreatment of black people, such as the Tuskegee Syphilis Study, has influenced this mistrust. There can be a fear that the medical profession not only does not have their best interests at heart but also that the system may actively be trying to harm them.

Are there any supplements that can be helpful?

There are claims that a variety of supplements and vitamins can help with mental health issues. There is limited research to support many of these. Studies have examined St. John's wort, and data have shown that it can be helpful for mild to moderate depression.[2] Melatonin has been shown to be helpful with sleep, and this will be discussed later in this chapter. Omega-3 fatty acids have shown to have some benefit with depressive disorders, including depression.[3] Studies have examined omega-3 fatty acids with postpartum depression and premenstrual mood disorders, along with major depressive disorder. S-Adenosyl-Methionine (SAM-e) is another compound that has been explored for depression. This may not be as practical because studies show that it is more helpful given via IV or injection into the muscle than with pills. The tricky thing is that the regulation of supplements varies greatly, so one needs to make sure that the supplement is of high enough quality to actually be helpful and that it does not contain any compounds that can be harmful. Every brand is not created equally. Also, it is important to let your doctor know what supplements you are taking so that he or she can make sure that other prescribed medications do not negatively interact with those supplements.

What is shock therapy?

The medical term for shock therapy is electroconvulsive therapy (ECT). Many have seen the movie *One Flew over the Cuckoo's Nest*, and ECT often appeared traumatic and scary in that movie. Keep in mind that Hollywood movies are designed to be dramatic. ECT is much safer and provided with much more care than was portrayed in that movie. In ECT, small electric currents go through the brain to trigger a brief, controlled seizure. This is done under anesthesia and under the close monitoring of multiple caregivers. The process has been further fine-tuned over the years to have fewer side effects, including decreased risk to memory. ECT is provided in a series of initial treatment sessions and can be used as a maintenance treatment to prevent symptom return after a patient has been stabilized on it. ECT has been known to be effective with high levels of symptom relief for a variety of psychiatric conditions.[4]

Why even use ECT?

ECT is indicated for use to treat bipolar disorder, major depressive disorder, and schizophrenia. ECT is an additional option for those who do not respond well to medication, either due to side effects or to the medication not working.

ECT sounds dangerous. Can it be used in the pregnant and the elderly?

ECT is used for older people to avoid side effects (the elderly can be more fragile) or to avoid severe interactions with their medications or other health conditions.[5] ECT has also been used to treat during pregnancy when there were concerns that ECT was safer than further treatment of medications. ECT is also the safest intervention during pregnancy.[6]

Is there something kind of like ECT without the shock?

A treatment called transmagnetic stimulation (TMS) has been developed as an alternative to ECT. TMS uses magnets to pass small electric currents to reset and affect brain cells, and it is also given in a series of treatments. One of the advantages of TMS is that it can be done without anesthesia and with less recovery time than ECT. TMS can also be done in a doctor's office.

John is a thirty-five-year-old African American gentleman and successful attorney. He is single but has a supportive network of family and friends. His best friends are ones who he has had since preschool. He was always a high achiever and always took pride in being a straight-A student. He always felt like he had a lot to lose because his parents had to work two jobs to allow him to go to a private school outside of his neighborhood, and then John worked while he was in college and law school. His goals have always included getting to a position where he could take care of his parents to repay them for all their dedication to him. Everything appeared to be going well until John's grades started going down during his freshman year in college. He started staying up for days at a time without any sleep. He found himself having a ton of energy and going from task to task to task. His friends started asking him what was up because they noticed he seemed more disorganized and was talking a mile a minute. They also kept telling him that they were not sure what he was talking about some of the time because he would go from subject to subject to subject in such a way that none of them could follow. They convinced him to go to the school health clinic, where he was referred to a psychiatrist. He was diagnosed with bipolar disorder and quickly stabilized with medication and psychotherapy. He got back on track quickly and has continued to do well with his treatment. He has always prioritized following up with his doctor and therapist regularly. At his most recent appointment, he brought up his concerns about weight gain from his medication. He felt that it had been working well, so he wanted to know if there was something he could do about the weight gain without stopping or changing his current medication.

How does what I eat affect my mental health?

Nutrition comes into the equation in a few different ways. There can be specific nutritional deficiencies that directly affect mood, including vitamin D deficiency. Also, overall malnutrition can affect mood. The body and mind need energy to work. If one's appetite is low or he or she is not eating much for other reasons, the body is deprived of fuel. The body needs a balanced diet to adequately keep everything moving in the right direction. For example, people can feel a crash after eating significant amounts of sugar or really heavy food. Also, the quality of food matters. The body needs real food. Processed food can also cause weight gain, sluggishness, and feelings of a crash of energy or even a change in mood after eating them. The other issue is that eating more is not necessarily equal to eating better. Emotional eating is a sneaky thing. You don't usually hear of people getting emotional food cravings for carrots and celery. The food cravings are often for sugar or dense carbohydrate/starchy foods (potatoes, chips, and the like). Also, overeating can sometimes make people feel sick. Emotional eating can be a way to feel comfort in the moment. Unfortunately, this comfort does not last. Afterward may follow the "food guilt" and feelings of sadness, especially when one has acknowledged that he or she has an issue with food or weight. In summary, the actual nutritional value of the food matters to adequately fuel the body, but the quantity of food matters to make sure that one is not consuming too little fuel or too much food, causing decreased energy, weight gain, and disappointment.

What is the role of nutrition? Is it more than just eating right?

Some nutrient deficiencies can affect mood, including vitamin D, folate, iron, and omega-3 fatty acids, but what is "eating right" to begin with? Often people mistake eating right for being on a diet. Healthy eating keeps in mind that the body and the mind need quality fuel. This quality fuel comes in the form of real food, not food made in a lab. If you need a chemistry degree to read a food label, then it is processed. Processed food can contain chemicals that are hard for your body to process, excess sugar, excess fats, and excess salt. Common things marked as "diet" foods or drinks often include artificial sweeteners, artificial fats, or other chemicals to make them tastier. The body has a hard time breaking down these chemicals. Also, a balanced diet that includes fruit, vegetables, protein, and some healthy fat will assist with obtaining the amount of vitamins and nutrients you need.

People talk about a healthy lifestyle. What does that mean?

The mind, body, and spirit are connected. People of color historically tend to have their physical bodies send signals that something is out of whack emotionally or spiritually. A simple example of this is when someone gets a headache or stomachache when he or she is feeling stressed. To function at our highest levels and to be our best selves, our minds, bodies, and spirits need to be aligned. If one is out of balance, the others may start to suffer. A healthy lifestyle is shorthand for adopting a mind-set of thoughts, habits, and behaviors that encourage our minds, bodies, and spirits to function well and to continue to move forward in personal, professional, and spiritual development that leads to peace, good health, and happiness along with self-love.

I hear about meditation, but what is it really, and what does it have to do with mental wellness?

Meditation often appears to be an unclear activity that is supposed to grant inner peace. Part of the reason it may seem like a vague concept is that there are a lot of ways to meditate. Meditation is a technique of calming the mind. Some techniques focus on quietly concentrating on a thought, feeling, or sensation, while others focus on having open thoughts but not reacting to them. An easy way to get started can be to use a guided meditation where someone talks you through the meditation. Other strategies include visualization, repeating a mantra, and being still and observing the sensations in the moment. All of them have in common achieving a calmer, quieter state of consciousness. Why does this matter? The ability to train one's mind is a powerful tool. This allows you to have a way to center and reset during stress, along with being less affected by the stress to begin with.

What is mindfulness, and why is it relevant?

Mindfulness is focusing your awareness in the present moment, including bodily sensations, thoughts, and feelings. Key concepts in mindfulness include acceptance and openness. With stress, along with numerous mental health conditions, the mind gets stuck worrying about the future, the past, or negative thoughts. Mindfulness pulls the mind to the present, which can break the cycle of these negative thoughts. In situations of addiction, mindfulness can also help interrupt thoughts that are focused on actively using addictive substances or negative thoughts that can trigger cravings. Being present in the moment also allows one to appreciate current positive experiences and sensations. Mindfulness has utility inside the setting of mental health and also in the context of everyday life.

Mindfulness is also used in reference to meditation, along with numerous therapies, including individual and group psychotherapies. Some additional programs include mindfulness-based stress reduction and mindfulness-based cognitive therapy, both of which use group therapy.[7]

Can yoga help too?

Yes, yoga can be an additional tool. Yoga assists in working on breathing, body awareness, and awareness of the mind, leading to increasing harmony of the mind and body. There are several types of yoga, so there are options that are more still and others, such as vinyasa, that are filled with more movement. Yoga is another strategy to help with reducing stress. It is an option that can also decrease having emotions on extra alert. For example, people with anxiety, including posttraumatic stress disorder, often feel on edge. Yoga can assist with decreasing being overly sensitive to emotions.

How does exercise make a difference?

Exercise plays a variety of roles in mental health, and there are plenty of theories behind how exercise can be helpful. For anxiety, exercise can mimic the bodily sensations felt when someone is anxious, causing those same sensations (muscle tension, sweating, increased heart rate) to be less trig-gering during an anxiety attack. Exercise can also assist with the release of endorphins (feel-good chemicals) in the brain. In addition, being active helps with sleep. The body was designed to be active. Exercise can also provide a sense of accomplishment and feeling of returning to normalcy.[8] There can be a sense of pride that you feel when you like the way you look. On the flip side of that, people can feel down when they gain weight or their clothes don't fit. Also, such health conditions as diabetes, high blood pressure, joint pain, and high cholesterol can respond well to exercise. These illnesses can impair quality of life and sometimes also negatively affect mood.

What about sleep?

Sleep plays a critical role in mental health. The body heals itself physically and emotionally during sleep. Without sleep, it is like the body is running on a low tank of fuel or driving around continuously with the check engine light on. Also, there are numerous mental health conditions that include insomnia as a major symptom.

Why should I consider something other than a sleeping pill?

There are numerous ways to treat problems of sleep, so it is good to know what your options are. Then you can work with your provider to choose the option that best fits your need. Some sleeping pills can be addictive. Also, sleeping pills can interact with other medications and other conditions, so it is helpful to be able to weigh different options.

What are things that can be done to assist with sleep?

Sleep hygiene is a fancy term for things that one can do to sleep better that do not include medication. Sleep hygiene includes going to bed at a consistent time, making the bed, not taking naps, avoiding caffeine in the evening, and having a nighttime routine. As painful as it may be, turning off electronics is also a powerful tool. The blue light in the screens stimulates the brain to be awake. Also, the beeps of notifications or the anticipation of a call, text, message, or other notification helps keep the body more alert. Smartphone apps can be used to assist in tracking sleep and can help when discussing sleep issues with a provider. They can be operated in do-not-disturb or sleep mode so that nighttime notifications can continue to be avoided. Also, numerous fitness monitors track sleep, and this information can be helpful to assist with figuring out what sleep interventions may be the most beneficial.

What if these strategies still don't have me feeling like my old self?

If none of these nonmedication options get you back to feeling like yourself, then you may need further assistance with medication or an adjustment to your current medication. Needing medication is not a weakness or a sign that you have failed. Medication is not a life sentence. Sometimes the biochemical nature of a mental health issue is enough that the body needs the help of medication to fight the chemical imbalance. Medication is another tool to assist people to get better, and the goal is for everyone to be able to enjoy life as their authentic selves.

The journey to mental wellness is not a one-size-fits-all treatment. Nonmedication treatments also provide additional tools to create a personalized plan to help each person live his or her best life and to feel healthy. These treatments can be used alone or in addition to other interventions, including medications. There are times when assumptions are made that African Americans may not have the psychological makeup, discipline, lifestyle, or support necessary to use nonmedication interventions. It is important for African Americans to be aware of a broad scope of treatments so that they can find the treatment strategy that best fits them.

Notes

1. David B. Larson, Kimberly A. Sherrill, John S. Lyons, Frederic C. Craigie Jr., Samuel B. Thielman, Mary A. Greenwold, and Susan S. Larson, "Associations between Dimensions of Religious Commitment and Mental Health Reported in the *American Journal of Psychiatry* and *Archives of General Psychiatry*: 1978–1989," *American Journal of Psychiatry* 149, no. 4 (1992): 557–59.

2. Klaus Linde, Gilbert Ramirez, Cynthia D. Mulrow, Andrej Pauls, Wolfgang Weidenhammer, and Dieter Melchart, "St John's Wort for Depression—An Overview and Meta-Analysis of Randomised Clinical Trials," *BMJ* 313, no. 7052 (1996): 253–58.

3. Alan C. Logan, "Omega-3 Fatty Acids and Major Depression: A Primer for the Mental Health Professional," *Lipids in Health and Disease* 3, no. 1 (2004): 25.

4. Nancy Kerner and Joan Prudic, "Current Electroconvulsive Therapy Practice and Research in the Geriatric Population," *Neuropsychiatry* 4, no. 1 (2014): 33–54.

5. Ibid.

6. Laura J. Miller, "Use of Electroconvulsive Therapy during Pregnancy," *Psychiatric Services* 45, no. 5 (1994): 444–50.

7. Hal Arkowitz and Scott O. Lilienfeld, "Is Mindfulness Good Medicine?" *Scientific American* 5, no. 25 (2014): 74–5.

8. Kirsten Weir, "The Exercise Effect," *Monitor on Psychology* 42, no. 11 (2011): 48.

CHAPTER 12

Racism and Inequalities in Mental Health Care

Aren't we in Post-Racial America?
MALAIKA BERKELEY, MD, MPH

What exactly is racism?

Racism is "A belief that one's own racial or ethnic group is superior, or that other such groups represent a threat to one's cultural identity, racial integrity, or economic well-being; Hence: prejudice, discrimination, or antagonism directed against people of other racial or ethnic groups especially based on such beliefs."[1] In other words, racism is prejudice against one racial or ethnic group by another. This prejudice is based on the belief that the offending group is superior to the others.

Does racism still exist?

Recent national information shows that Whites are hesitant to admit to positive stereotypes of Blacks and that negative stereotypes of minority groups are common. Although Whites have negative views of all minority groups, Blacks are viewed more negatively than any other group. National data indicate the following:[2]

- Forty-five percent of Whites believe that most Blacks are lazy.
- Fifty-one percent of Whites believe that most Blacks are prone to violence.
- Twenty-nine percent of Whites believe that most Blacks are not intelligent.
- Fifty-six percent of Whites believe that Blacks prefer to live off welfare.
- Only 17 percent of Whites indicated that most Blacks are hardworking.
- Only 15 percent of Whites indicated that most Blacks are not prone to violence.
- Only 21 percent of Whites indicated that most Blacks are intelligent.
- Only 12 percent of Whites indicated that most Blacks prefer to be self-supporting.

What are health-care inequalities?

It is well known that there are noticeable differences in the health and healthcare received by Blacks and other minorities as compared to Whites. These minorities include African Americans, Hispanic Americans, American Indians, Asian Americans, and Native Hawaiians/Other Pacific Islanders.

These minorities have been noted generally to die at an earlier age and to suffer in greater numbers and severity from such illnesses and events as diabetes, cancer, heart disease, substance abuse, and infant deaths. In addition, there are obvious differences in minorities' abilities to receive quality care and sometimes any care at all. These differences in health and health care are known as healthcare disparities.

Inequalities have been found to occur based on age, social standing, wealth, location, language, gender, sexual identity, and orientation.[3] However, it has been shown that inequalities due to race and ethnicity exist even if all other factors are the same.[4]

How does racism play a role in inequalities?

Racism is as difficult to identify in the medical field as it is in the general population because it generally requires admission by the offending party. However, as noted earlier, we have come to realize that even when all else is equal in two patients, their health care tends to differ simply based on race. It has been shown that there tend to be differences in the way medicine is practiced when treating minority versus nonminority patients. These differences in practices have been shown to not be based on medical science.

Which health conditions are affected by inequalities?

Health inequalities affect minorities in almost all health conditions even including dental care. The following are just a few examples:[5]

- Deaths from heart diseases occur at a rate of 252 per 100,000 in African Americans compared to 206 per 100,000 in Whites.
- Blacks are more than twice as likely to be diagnosed with diabetes than Whites.
- Blacks are almost 1.25 times as likely to die due to cancer than Whites.
- Infant deaths occur more than twice as often in Blacks than in Whites.
- End-stage renal disease occurs four times more often in Blacks than in Whites.
- AIDS is diagnosed more than seven times as often in Black males than in White males and twenty-four times as often in Black females than in White females.

How does racism affect mental health?

The former United States Surgeon General, Dr. David Satcher, issued a report in 2001 that detailed the effects of race and inequalities on mental health. He noted three major ways that racism affects the *mental health of minorities*. *These include the following:*[6]

- Racism and discrimination can directly lead to depression, substance abuse, and physical health problems.
- Being faced with negative stereotypes and images can reduce the self-esteem of minorities and negatively affect their mental health.
- Racism has led to higher levels of poverty, crime, and violence in the African American community. This can in turn lead to higher levels of depression, substance abuse, and trauma-related mental health conditions

What inequalities exist in mental health care?

Disparities exist between Whites and minorities in the ability to access care, the accuracy of diagnosis, and the manner and type of treatment provided. It has been noted that racial and ethnic minorities with mental conditions consistently have less access to care, receive lower quality services, and leave treatment at a higher rate than nonminority colleagues.[7] We will discuss these in more detail next.

What causes inequalities in getting mental health care?

Stigma, homelessness, high unemployment rates, lower insurance rates, and unequal pay affect minorities' ability to get mental health care.

Stigma causes individuals to fear, reject, avoid, and discriminate against people with mental illness. African Americans fear mental health treatment due to stigma more than twice as much as Whites. African Americans are also more likely to believe their symptoms are spiritually based and are more likely to first seek help from clergy, traditional healers, family, and friends. When African Americans do seek professional assistance for mental health symptoms, they are more likely than Whites to seek help from primary care providers than from mental health specialists.[8]

Inequalities have been noted not only in the rates at which African American patients enter treatment but also the rates at which they remain in treatment. They often leave treatment after the first visit. It is unclear if mistrust is the reason for this occurrence. However, it is well understood that African Americans are hesitant to trust providers based on a history of mistreatment as well as current experiences of racism. In fact African Americans and Latinos were more than ten times more likely than Whites to feel unfairly judged or disrespected by a provider due to their race.[9]

African Americans make up 40 percent of the homeless population, a rate 3.5 times that of the white homeless population. The homeless population generally does not voluntarily seek care but is usually brought to others' attention once they violate some law.[10]

Nearly one-quarter of African Americans are uninsured, one and a half times the rate of Whites.[11]

Greater than one in five African American families have incomes below the poverty line compared to one in ten of all American families. The African American rate of severe poverty is more than three times that of the white rate.[12] Minorities also tend to occupy poorer and more rural communities, relying more heavily on public transportation than more wealthy communities. All these factors make it more difficult for African Americans to get the care they need.

What causes inequalities in mental health diagnosis?

In psychiatry above all other fields of medicine, understanding an individual's culture is essential to identifying (diagnosing) his or her condition. A patient's symptoms must always be compared to the general thinking within that individual's culture. For this reason, it is generally true that minorities stand a better chance of getting a correct diagnosis if they are treated by others from a similar culture.

Understanding a patient's culture can make the difference in a patient's mistrust being labeled as paranoia versus a cultural norm. In fact, occurrences like this are thought to be part of the reason that African Americans are diagnosed with schizophrenia and psychotic disorders at higher rates when diagnosed by non-minorities.[13]

Most mental health professionals use certain books and tests to identify an individual's condition. These include the *Diagnostic and Statistical Manual of Mental Disorders* (DSM-5) and other standardized tests. Many times these are thought to be culturally biased toward the language and values of White Americans.[14] Since, the language used by minorities does not always match perfectly with that of these tests and books, a culturally inexperienced practitioner can easily misdiagnose a minority patient.

What are the inequalities in mental health treatment?

It has been shown that there are greater numbers of African Americans than Whites in psychiatric emergency rooms and inpatient hospitals. African Americans are also more likely than Whites to be brought to the emergency room by the police and to be admitted to the hospital against their will.[15] This may be due in part to the greater fear of psychiatric treatment experienced by African Americans, along with lower rates of insurance and other issues that affect their ability to get routine care.

When African Americans do receive treatment, they are more likely to receive inferior treatment for depression and anxiety. For example, only twenty-seven out of every one hundred African Americans were likely to receive antidepressants when first diagnosed with depression compared with forty-four out of every one hundred Caucasians.[16]

When African Americans do receive psychiatric treatment, they are also more likely than Whites to receive antipsychotic medication and more likely to receive these antipsychotics involuntarily by injection. African Americans are also more likely to receive older antipsychotics and higher doses than Whites.[17] This practice puts African Americans at greater risk of developing medication side effects.

Greater than a third of all prisoners in state and federal prisons are African American[18] as are 40 percent of juveniles in residential custody facilities.[19] Mental illness exists at high rates in prisons and jails. As in the general public, incarcerated African Americans are less likely than incarcerated Whites to receive psychiatric care.[20]

What are people doing to address disparities?

There are several medical and public health agencies and task forces actively working to better understand the causes of health and health-care inequalities. This is viewed as the first step toward addressing and reducing these inequalities. Recommendations are coming in slowly but include the following:[21]

- Using proven effective treatment in all populations
- Increasing the number of African American mental health providers
- Reducing the stigma of mental health care
- Providing grants for research within the minority community that is spearheaded and conducted by minority providers
- Making healthcare disparities required learning for providers in training

Other useful recommendations may include addressing the larger issue of racism, which would help the minority communities in many ways, including the following:

- Lowering unemployment rates
- Lowering rates of homelessness
- Increasing household incomes
- Increasing rates of health-care insurance
- Increasing ability to access health care
- Reducing noise and overcrowding in homes
- Reducing violence in communities

- Reducing conditions caused by poor living environments
- Reducing incarcerations
- Increasing self-esteem
- Making America great for everyone

What can I do to reduce disparities?

By purchasing this book, you have already taken the first step. Lack of sufficient health information is a key factor in disparities. Becoming more informed about mental health conditions will help guide you in knowing when you should see your health-care provider. Many times behaviors are thought to be within an individual's control. An individual may be thought to be "acting out" or just behaving badly, when in fact that person may be in need of professional help. If you are in doubt, it doesn't hurt to do some research.

Knowing where to go to get help for you or your loved one can be an additional hurdle; however, technology has almost eliminated this barrier. Whether you have an Internet-capable phone or computer at home or you need to go to your local library for Internet access, information on nearby providers can easily be found. You may call or go to your insurance provider's website or simply go to any search engine to locate a provider near you.

Finally, taking that brave step for yourself or supporting your loved one in taking that step to seek treatment will get you on your way to understanding what is happening and moving toward recovery.

So, arm yourself with knowledge, use the resources available to assist you, and get the help you need with little delay. Help us reduce health-care inequalities one person at a time.

Notes

1. "Racism," *Oxford English Dictionary*, accessed January 29, 2017, http://www.oed.com.
2. "Causes of Health Disparities," University of Minnesota, accessed January 29, 2017, http://www.epi.umn.edu/let/nutri/disparities/causes.shtm.

3. "Disparities in Health and Health Care: Five Key Questions and Answers," Petry Ubri and Samantha Artiga, Henry J. Kaiser Family Foundation, accessed January 29, 2017, http://kff.org/disparities-policy/issue-brief/disparities-in-health-and-health-care-five-key-questions-and-answers/.

4. Lonnie R. Snowden, "Bias in Mental Health Assessment and Intervention: Theory and Evidence," *American Journal of Public Health* 93, no. 2 (2003): 239–43.

5. "NIH Health Disparities Strategic Plan, Fiscal Years 2004–2008, Volume 1," National Institutes of Health and US Department of Health and Human Services, accessed February 8, 2018, https://www.nimhd.nih.gov/docs/2004_2008_strategic_plan_vol1.pdf.

6. US Department of Health and Human Services, *Mental Health: Culture, Race, and Ethnicity—A Supplement to Mental Health: A Report of the Surgeon General* (Rockville, MD: US Department of Health and Human Services, 2001).

7. "Closing the Gaps: Reducing Disparities in Mental Health Treatment through Engagement," National Institute of Mental Health, accessed January 29, 2017, https://www.nimh.nih.gov/research-priorities/scientific-meetings/2011/closing-the-gaps-reducing-disparities-in-mental-health-treatment-through-engagement/index.shtml.

8. US Department of Health and Human Services, *Mental Health*.

9. Ibid.

10. Ibid.

11. Ibid.

12. Ibid.

13. Malaika E. Berkeley, "Patient 24," in *Psychiatry Pearls*, by Alex Kolevzon and Daniel G. Stewart (Philadelphia: Hanley & Belfus, 2004), 83–7.

14. Sylvia Atdjian and William A.Vega, "Disparities in Mental Health Treatment in US Racial and Ethnic Minority Groups: Implications for Psychiatrists," *Psychiatric Services* 56, no. 12 (2005): 1600–02.

15. Snowden, "Bias in Mental Health Assessment and Intervention."

16. US Department of Health and Human Services, *Mental Health*.

17. Snowden, "Bias in Mental Health Assessment and Intervention."

18. "Estimated Number of Sentenced Prisoners under State and Federal Jurisdiction, by Sex, Race, Hispanic Origin, and Age," Bureau of Justice Statistics, accessed January 13, 2018, https://www.bjs.gov/index.cfm?ty=nps.

19. "Juveniles in Public and Private Residential Custody Facilities, by Race, Ethnicity, and Offense, United States," Sourcebook of Criminal Justice Statistics, accessed January 13, 2018, https://www.albany.edu/source-book/tost_6.html#6_b.

20. US Department of Health and Human Services, *Mental Health*.

21. Institute of Medicine, *Unequal Treatment: Confronting Racial and Ethnic Disparities in Health Care* (Washington, DC: The National Acadamies Press, 2003).

CHAPTER 13
Summary: Psychiatry with Love

NAPOLEON B. HIGGINS JR., MD

The purpose of this book is so that individuals, families, and communities who are affected by mental illness can better understand it. Too often psychiatry, mental health, and mental illness are poorly understood and feared in the Black communities. We hope that this book will help to fill some of the gaps between the mental health community and this culturally diverse and important group within our American culture. Mental health is a part of an individual's overall health. Depression, sadness, anxiety, mood swings, and addiction are all treatable with a combination of self-care, lifestyle changes, and, sometimes, medication management. The mind and brain are attached to the body and, just like any part of the body, can have problems; so does the brain. When the brain is ill, it will change how we feel, behave, and react to our environment.

Good outcomes are primarily dependent on prevention, early recognition, understanding of the issues, and willingness to receive care and perform the necessary steps and changes to get better. Another integral part to healing is the support of loved ones and the community. It is our hope that this book will help spread the word about mental health, wellness, and how to get help. It is designed to serve as a resource for individuals and communities so that the reader will be able to clearly understand the book and share with others. It is written so that consumers, families, and communities, including churches, social workers, police, and policymakers, can have a better understanding of mental health.

The most common face of illness is not someone who looks outwardly ill; the most common face of mental illness is a person who looks like you or me. On the outside people can't see the pain others are going through. The pain is internal and deep within, but the pain doesn't have to stay there. There is hope, there is treatment, and there are mental health professionals out there who are ready to help and to see you as a whole person.

Lastly, but most importantly, this has been a project of love for our community among highly trained professionals from the same community. We all have very busy lives as physicians, but we all took the time to help the community by writing a book that could reach well beyond the walls of our practices. We are from the community, and we are giving back to the community. Most importantly, this is a project fueled by love, and we hope this book enhances lives, families, and communities. This book is truly about *love* for our community. Too often these books are written for psychiatrists and other professionals and not for the people who need it most—the patients and families who are suffering with these issues. The client, family, and community are the focus of this book.

This book is *psychiatry with love* for the community to promote *mental health for the people!*

APPENDIX A: EVERYTHING YOU WANTED TO KNOW
ABOUT PSYCHIATRY BUT WERE AFRAID TO ASK

JAMES LEE JR., MD

"If I go see a psychiatrist, people are going to think I'm crazy."

Throughout this book, we have taken a very straightforward approach to explaining various psychiatric disorders. However, we realize that there are just as many questions prior to an appointment as there are after the appointment is completed. This appendix attempts to answer some of those questions. In doing so, we hope to put everyone at ease as they start the process of getting the help they need.

How do I find a psychiatrist or mental health provider?

There are several options when trying to find a provider. Most providers are still listed in the phonebook. However, any listing in the phonebook can be searched online through Google, Bing, or any other search engine. Also, your insurance company can give you information on local doctors who are in network.

What does it mean if a doctor is out of network?

If a doctor is out of network, he or she does not have a contract with your insurance company, and they may not pay for your visit. Not all doctors accept insurance, and some operate only on cash payments. However, there are doctors who accept insurance. They will accept the payment from your insurance company. Many doctors are now requiring you to pay your portion of the visit (copay or coinsurance) up front prior to being seen.

What do I need to bring to my appointment?

Most doctors need to know any current medications you are taking, along with the dosages. If you don't have a list already prepared, your pharmacy will be able to provide this for you. It also helps to have a list of current medical problems you are being treated for by other physicians. In addition, it is important to tell your doctor about any over-the-counter medications or supplements you are taking.

What should I expect for the first appointment?

You and your doctor will talk for approximately forty to sixty minutes about your previous psychiatric problems and current concerns. Some doctors allow you to talk and ask very few questions, while others ask most of the questions to make sure they get all the information needed to make an accurate diagnosis.

I don't want the doctor to think that I am crazy. Do I have to tell him or her everything?

It is helpful to be honest and open with your doctor. The only way the doctor can truly help you is to know what is going on. The doctor is not there to judge you, only to help you address your problems and concerns.

If I go see a psychiatrist, will he or she lock me up?

Most visits to a psychiatrist *do not* result in you being admitted to the hospital. The doctor will ask you questions about your safety and the safety of others. If the psychiatrist feels that you may be at risk or someone else may be in danger due to your actions or urges, he or she may discuss the option of hospitalization.

Is it OK to bring someone to the appointment with me?

Most doctors will allow you to have a family member or friend join you in the appointment. However, due to certain laws (such as HIPAA), you have to give permission for the person to come into the appointment. Most offices are not equipped for an entire family to join you. Contact the office directly and ask about its policy before attending the appointment.

If I tell the doctor everything, will he or she tell my business to others?

The doctors as well as the staff within the office are held to a high standard when it comes to releasing information. When you are in the office, none of the information you discuss with the doctor can be shared without your permission (this is called confidentiality). Failure to follow these rules can cause the staff as well as the doctor to get into trouble.

Will the psychiatrist talk with my regular doctor about my case?

The psychiatrist can talk to other doctors concerning your case if you give him or her permission. However, in the case of an emergency, permission is not needed. Most doctors have forms (called informed consent) that you fill out to either give them permission to talk to other doctors or to request information from these doctors to better assist them with your treatment.

What happens after I talk with the psychiatrist?

After the initial appointment, the psychiatrist will give you his or her impression of what is going on at this time (the diagnosis). There may be more than one diagnosis, or the doctor may be working to rule out a certain diagnosis. Next, the doctor will talk about options for treatment. Usually, these options are medications, counseling/therapy, or both. The doctor's recommendation is usually based on the diagnosis and how severe your symptoms may be.

Do I have to take medications every day?

Most medications prescribed for psychiatric purposes are taken every day. Some medications are prescribed on an as-needed basis. These medications are typically used only when a problem is present. It is important to follow the doctor's instructions regarding taking your medications.

Will these medications have side effects?

All medications have potential side effects. However, it is not a definite that you will have problems from any of the listed side effects. Most individuals experience side effects within the first few days, and then the problems go away. If the problems continue for a longer time period, contact your doctor to discuss whether this medication is the right one for you. One rule of thumb most doctors will relay to their patients is that side effects are possibilities, not probabilities.

How often do I have to see the psychiatrist?

The frequency of treatments is based on the doctor's comfort level with you at the time of the appointment. If you are not doing as well and a recent change was made to your medication, the doctor might see you within days to weeks. However, if you are stable on your current medications, your appointment might be closer to two to three months. Each doctor has a different level of comfort when scheduling follow-up appointments.

APPENDIX B: COMMONLY USED MEDICATIONS

KARRIEM L. SALAAM, MD

Medicines used to treat attention deficit hyperactivity disorder:

- methylphenidate (Ritalin/Concerta)
- dexmethylphenidate (Focalin)
- dextroamphetamine (Dexedrine)
- mixed amphetamine salts (Adderall)
- atomoxetine (Strattera)

Medicines used to treat anxiety:

- alprazolam (Xanax)
- buspirone (Buspar)
- clonazepam (Klonopin)
- diazepam (Valium)
- lorazepam (Ativan)

Medicines used to treat depression:

- bupropion (Wellbutrin)
- escitalopram (Lexapro)
- fluoxetine (Prozac)
- paroxetine (Paxil)
- sertraline (Zoloft)
- venlafaxine (Effexor)

Medicines used to treat aggression or changes in mood:

- aripiprazole (Abilify)
- carbamazepine (Tegretol)

- oxcarbazepine (Trileptal)
- lamotrigine (Lamictal)
- lithium (Eskalith, Lithobid)
- valproic acid (Depakote)

Medicines used to treat disorganized thoughts, behaviors, and voices:

- chlorpromazine (Thorazine)
- haloperidol (Haldol)
- olanzapine (Zyprexa)
- risperidone (Risperdal)
- ziprasidone (Geodon)
- clozapine (Clozaril)

BIBLIOGRAPHY

Introduction

American Psychiatric Association. *Diagnostic and Statistical Manual of Mental Disorders*. 5th ed. Washington, DC: American Psychiatric Association, 2013.

Chapter 2

American Psychiatric Association. "Depressive Disorders." In *Desk Reference to the Diagnostic Criteria from DSM-5*. Washington, DC: American Psychiatric Association, 2013.

American Psychiatric Association. "What Is Depression?" Ranna Parekh. Accessed December 12, 2017. https://www.psychiatry.org/patients-families/depression/what-is-depression.

CNN. "Suicide Rates among Young Black Boys on the Rise." Carina Storrs. May 19, 2015. http://www.cnn.com/2015/05/19/health/suicide-youth/index.html.

Depression and Bipolar Support Alliance. "About the Depression and Bipolar Support Alliance." Accessed December 12, 2017, http://www.dbsalliance.org/site/PageServer?pagename=dbsa_about_dbsa.

Freimuth, Vicki S., Sandra Crouse Quinn, Stephen B. Thomas, Galen Cole, Eric Zook, and Ted Duncan. "African Americans' Views on Research and the Tuskegee Syphilis Study." *Social Science & Medicine* 52, no. 5 (2001): 797–808.

Gamble, Vanessa Northington. "Under the Shadow of Tuskegee: African Americans and Health Care." *American Journal of Public Health* 87, no. 11 (1997): 1773–78.

Givens, Jane L., Ira R. Katz, Scarlett Bellamy, and William C. Holmes. "Stigma and the Acceptability of Depression Treatments among African Americans and Whites." *Journal of General Internal Medicine* 22, no. 9 (2007): 1292–97.

Jackson, Leslie C., and Beverly Greene, eds. *Psychotherapy with African American Women: Innovations in Psychodynamic Perspectives and Practice.* New York: The Guilford Press, 2000.

Joe, Sean, Briggett C. Ford, Robert Joseph Taylor, and Linda M. Chatters. "Prevalence of Suicide Ideation and Attempts among Black Americans in Later Life." *Transcultural Psychiatry* 51, no. 2 (2014): 190–208.

Kessler, Ronald C., Patricia Berglund, Olga Demler, Robert Jin, Kathleen R. Merikangas, and Ellen E. Walters. "Lifetime Prevalence and Age of Onset Distributions of *DSM-IV* Disorders in the National Comorbidity Survey Replication." *Archives of General Psychiatry* 62, no. 6 (2005): 593–602.

Matthews, Alicia K., Patrick Corrigan, Barbara M. Smith, and Frances Aranda. "A Qualitative Exploration of African-Americans' Attitudes toward Mental Illness and Mental Illness Treatment Seeking." *Journal of the National Council on Rehabilitation Education* 20, no. 4 (2006): 253–68.

Mayo Clinic. "Depression (Major Depressive Disorder)." Mayo Clinic Staff. Accessed December 12, 2017. https://www.mayoclinic.org/diseases-conditions/depression/symptoms-causes/syc-20356007.

National Alliance on Mental Illness. "About NAMI." Accessed December 12, 2017, https://www.nami.org/About-NAMI.

Neighbors, Harold W., Cleopatra Caldwell, David R. Williams, Randolph Nesse, Robert Joseph Taylor, Kai McKeever Bullard, Myriam Torres, and James S. Jackson. "Race, Ethnicity, and the Use of Services for Mental

Disorders: Results from the National Survey of American Life." *Archives of General Psychiatry* 64, no. 4 (2007): 485–94.

Poussaint, Alvin F., and Amy Alexander. *Lay My Burden Down: Suicide and the Mental Health Crisis among African Americans*. Boston, MA: Beacon Press, 2000.

Schnittker, Jason. "Misgivings of Medicine? African Americans' Skepticism of Psychiatric Medication." *Journal of Health and Social Behavior* 44, no. 4 (2003): 506–24.

Schraufnagel, Trevor J., Amy W. Wagner, Jeanne Miranda, and Peter P. Roy-Byrne. "Treating Minority Patients with Depression and Anxiety: What Does the Evidence Tell Us?" *General Hospital Psychiatry* 28, no. 4 (2006): 517–27.

West, Lindsey M., Roxanne A. Donovan, and Amanda R. Daniel. "The Price of Strength: Black College Women's Perspectives on the Strong Black Woman Stereotype." *Women & Therapy* 39, nos. 3–4 (2016): 390–412.

Whiteford, Harvey A., Louisa Degenhardt, Jürgen Rehm, Amanda J. Baxter, Alize J. Ferrari, Holly E. Erskine, Fiona J. Charlson, et al. "Global Burden of Disease Attributable to Mental and Substance Use Disorders: Findings from the Global Burden of Disease Study 2010." *The Lancet* 382, no. 9904 (2013): 1575–86.

Williams, David R., Hector M. Gonzalez, Harold Neighbors, Randolph Nesse, Jamie M. Abelson, Julie Sweetman, and James S. Jackson. "Prevalence and Distribution of Major Depressive Disorder in African Americans, Caribbean Blacks, and Non-Hispanic Whites: Results from the National Survey of American Life." *Archives of General Psychiatry* 64, no. 3 (2007): 305–15.

Wingfield, Adia Harvey. "The Modern Mammy and the Angry Black Man: African American Professionals' Experiences with Gendered Racism in the Workplace." *Race, Gender & Class* 14, nos. 1/2 (2007): 196–212.

Wynia, Matthew K., and Vanessa Northington Gamble. "Mistrust among Minorities and the Trustworthiness Medicine." *PLoS Medicine* 3, no. 5 (2006): e244.

Chapter 3

American Psychiatric Association. *Diagnostic and Statistical Manual of Mental Disorders.* 5th ed. Washington, DC: American Psychiatric Association, 2013.

Bauer, Mark, Jürgen Unützer, Harold A. Pincus, and William B. Lawson. "Bipolar Disorder." *Mental Health Services Research* 4, no. 4 (2002): 225–29.

Bell, Carl C., and Radhika Chimata. "Prevalence of Neurodevelopmental Disorders among Low-Income African Americans at a Clinic on Chicago's South Side." *Psychiatric Services* 66, no. 5 (2015): 539–42.

Colom, Francesco, Eduard Vieta, Anabel Martínez-Arán, María Reinares, José Manuel Goikolea, Antonio Benabarre, Carla Torrent, et al. "A Randomized Trial on the Efficacy of Group Psychoeducation in the Prophylaxis of Recurrences in Bipolar Patients Whose Disease Is in Remission." *Archives of General Psychiatry* 60, no. 4 (2003): 402–07.

Henderson, David C. "Weight Gain with Atypical Antipsychotics: Evidence and Insights." *The Journal of Clinical Psychiatry* 68, suppl. 12 (2006): 18–26.

Hirschfeld, Robert, and Lana A. Vornik. "Perceptions and Impact of Bipolar Disorder: How Far Have We Really Come? Results of the National Depressive and Manic-Depressive Association 2000 Survey of Individuals with Bipolar Disorder." *The Journal of Clinical Psychiatry* 64, no. 2 (2003): 402–07.

Jain, Rakesh, Vladimir Maletic, and Roger S. McIntyre. "Diagnosing and Treating Patients with Mixed Features." *The Journal of Clinical Psychiatry* 78, no. 8 (2017): 1091–1102.

Lachar, David, Sonja L. Randle, Andrew Harper, Kathy C. Scott-Gurnell, Kay R. Lewis, Cynthia W. Santos, Ann E. Saunders, Deborah A. Pearson, Katherine A. Loveland, and Sharon T. Morgan. "The Brief Psychiatric Rating Scale for Children (BPRS-C): Validity and Reliability of an Anchored Version." *Journal of the American Academy of Child & Adolescent Psychiatry* 40, no. 3 (2001): 333–40.

Sylvia, Louisa G., Stephanie Salcedo, Emily E. Bernstein, Ji Hyun Baek, Andrew A. Nierenberg, and Thilo Deckersbach. "Nutrition, Exercise, and Wellness Treatment in Bipolar Disorder: Proof of Concept for a Consolidated Intervention." *International Journal of Bipolar Disorders* 1, no. 1 (2013): 1–24.

Wagner, Karen Dineen, Robert M. A. Hirschfeld, Graham Emslie, Robert Findling, Barbara L. Gracious, and Michael L. Reed. "Validation of the Mood Disorder Questionnaire for Bipolar Disorders in Adolescents." *The Journal of Clinical Psychiatry* 67, no. 5 (2006): 827–30.

Chapter 4

American Psychiatric Association. *Diagnostic and Statistical Manual of Mental Disorders*. 5th ed. Washington, DC: American Psychiatric Association, 2013.

Leichsenring, Falk, and Christiane Steinert. "Is Cognitive Behavioral Therapy the Gold Standard for Psychotherapy? The Need for Plurality in

Treatment and Research." *Journal of the American Medical Association* 318, no. 14 (2017): 1323–24.

National Alliance on Mental Illness. "Anxiety Disorders." Accessed February 8, 2018. https://www.nami.org/Learn-More/Mental-Health-Conditions/Anxiety-Disorders.

National Institute of Mental Health. "Anxiety Disorders." Accessed February 8, 2018. https://www.nimh.nih.gov/health/topics/anxiety-disorders/index.shtml.

Chapter 5

American Psychiatric Association. *Diagnostic and Statistical Manual of Mental Disorders.* 5th ed. Washington, DC: American Psychiatric Association, 2013.

Boel-Studt, Shamra Marie. "A Quasi-Experimental Study of Trauma-Informed Psychiatric Residential Treatment for Children and Adolescents." *Research on Social Work Practice* 27, no. 3 (2017): 273–82.

Breslau, Naomi. "Trauma and Mental Health in US Inner-City Populations." *General Hospital Psychiatry* 31, no. 6 (2009): 501–02.

Perrin, Sean. "Children Exposed to Trauma Should Be Screened for Symptoms of PTSD." *Evidence-Based Mental Health* 17, no. 4 (2014): 107.

Rideout, Leslie C., and Patricia A. Normandin. "Pediatric Post-Traumatic Stress Disorder." *Journal of Emergency Nursing* 41, no. 6 (2015): 531–32.

Chapter 6

American Psychiatric Association. *Diagnostic and Statistical Manual of Mental Disorders.* 5th ed. Washington, DC: American Psychiatric Association, 2013.

Chong, Heuy Yi, Siew Li Teoh, David Bin-Chia Wu, Surachai Kotirium, Chiun-Fang Chiou, and Nathorn Chaiyakunapruk. "Global Economic Burden of Schizophrenia: A Systematic Review." *Neuropsychiatric Disease and Treatment* 12 (2016): 357–73.

Dean, Kimberlie, and Robin M. Murray. "Environmental Risk Factors for Psychosis." *Dialogues in Clinical Neuroscience* 7, no. 1 (2005): 69–80.

The Internet Mental Health Initiative. "Schizophrenia Facts and Statistics." Assessed January 12, 2018. http://www.schizophrenia.com/szfacts.htm.

Kane, John M., and Christoph U. Correll. "Pharmacologic Treatment of Schizophrenia." *Dialogues in Clinical Neuroscience* 12, no. 3 (2010): 345–57.

Lawrie, Stephen M., Bayanne Olabi, Jeremy Hall, and Andrew M. McIntosh. "Do We Have Any Solid Evidence of Clinical Utility about the Pathophysiology of Schizophrenia?" *World Psychiatry* 10, no. 1 (2011): 19–31.

McGrath, Barbara Burns, and Karen L. Edwards. "When Family Means More (or Less) Than Genetics: The Intersection of Culture, Family, and Genomics." *Journal of Transcultural Nursing* 20, no. 3 (2009): 270–77.

Mental Health America. "Psychosis (Schizophrenia) in Children and Youth." Accessed January 12, 2018. http://www.mentalhealthamerica.net/conditions/psychosis-schizophrenia-children-and-youth.

National Alliance on Mental Health. "Early Psychosis and Psychosis." Assessed January 13, 2018. https://www.nami.org/earlypsychosis.

National Institute of Mental Illness. "Schizophrenia." Assessed January 12, 2018. https://www.nimh.nih.gov/health/topics/schizophrenia/index.shtml.

Picchioni, Marco M., and Robin Murray. "Schizophrenia." *BMJ* 335, no. 7610 (2007): 91–5.

Schizophrenia.com. "The Causes of Schizophrenia." Accessed January 12, 2018. http://schizophrenia.com/hypo.php.

Schizophrenia.com. "The Importance of Early Treatment for Schizophrenia and Psychosis." Accessed May 8, 2014. http://schizophrenia.com/?p=406.

Schultz, Stephen H., Stephen W. North, and Cleveland G. Shields. "Schizophrenia: A Review." *American Family Physician* 75, no. 12 (2007): 1821–29.

Schwartz, Robert C., and David M. Blankenship. "Racial Disparities in Psychotic Disorder Diagnosis: A Review of Empirical Literature," *World Journal of Psychiatry* 4, no. 4 (2014): 133–40.

UpToDate. "Pharmacotherapy for Schizophrenia: Acute and Maintenance Phase Treatment." T. Scott Stroup and Stephen Marder. Last updated May 23, 2017. https://www.uptodate.com/contents/pharmacotherapy-for-schizophrenia-acute-and-maintenance-phase-treatment.

Wildgust, Hiram Joseph, Richard Hodgson, and Mike Beary. "The Paradox of Premature Mortality in Schizophrenia: New Research Questions." *Journal of Psychopharmacology* 24, no. 4 (2010): 9–15.

Zen Psychiatry. "Think You're Going Crazy? A Beginner's Guide to Psychosis." Elana Miller. October 20, 2011. http://zenpsychiatry.com/beginners-guide-to-psychosis/.

Chapter 7
Alavi, Seyyed Salman, Masoud Ferdosi, Fereshte Jannatifard, Mehdi Eslami, Hamed Alaghemandan, and Mehrdad Setare. "Behavioral Addiction

versus Substance Addiction: Correspondence of Psychiatric and Psychological Views." *International Journal of Preventive Medicine* 3, no. 4 (2012): 290–94.

American Psychiatric Association. *Diagnostic and Statistical Manual of Mental Disorders.* 5th ed. Washington, DC: American Psychiatric Association, 2013.

Budney, Alan J., Roger Roffman, Robert S. Stephens, and Denise Walker. "Marijuana Dependence and Its Treatment." *Addiction Science & Clinical Practice* 4, no. 1 (2007): 4–16.

Center for Behavioral Health Statistics and Quality. *Behavioral Health Trends in the United States: Results from the 2014 National Survey on Drug Use and Health.* Rockville, MD: Center for Behavioral Health Statistics and Quality, Substance Abuse and Mental Health Services Administration, 2015.

Fowler, Joanna S., Nora D. Volkow, Cheryl A. Kassed, and Linda Chang. "Imaging the Addicted Human Brain." *Science & Practice Perspectives* 3, no. 2 (2007): 4–16.

Hasin, Deborah S., Tulshi D. Saha, Bradley T. Kerridge, Risë B. Goldstein, S. Patricia Chou, Haitao Zhang, Jeesun Jung, et al. "Prevalence of Marijuana Use Disorders in the United States between 2001–2002 and 2012–2013." *JAMA Psychiatry* 72, no. 12 (2015): 1235–42.

National Center on Addiction and Substance Abuse at Columbia University. *Behind Bars II: Substance Abuse and America's Prison Population.* New York: National Center on Addiction and Substance Abuse at Columbia University, 2010.

National Institute on Alcohol Abuse and Alcoholism. "NIAAA Council Approves Definition of Binge Drinking." *NIAAA Newsletter* 3 (Winter 2004): 3.

National Institute on Drug Abuse. "Drugs, Brains, and Behavior: The Science of Addiction." Accessed January 15, 2018. https://www.drugabuse.gov/publications/drugs-brains-behavior-science-addiction.

National Institute on Drug Abuse. "Treatment Approaches for Drug Addiction." Accessed January 15, 2018. https://www.drugabuse.gov/publications/drugfacts/treatment-approaches-drug-addiction.

National Institute on Drug Abuse. "Treatment Statistics." Accessed January 7, 2018. https://www.drugabuse.gov/publications/drugfacts/treatment-statistics.

National Institute on Drug Abuse. "Trends & Statistics." Accessed January 15, 2018. https://www.drugabuse.gov/related-topics/trends-statistics.

National Institute on Drug Abuse. "Understanding Drug Use and Addiction." Accessed January 15, 2018. https://www.drugabuse.gov/publications/drugfacts/understanding-drug-use-addiction.

Ramasundarahettige, Prabhat Jha Chinthanie, Victoria Landsman, Brian Rostron, Michael Thun, Robert Anderson, Tim McAfee, and Richard Peto. "21st Century Hazards of Smoking and Benefits of Cessation in the United States." *New England Journal of Medicine* 368 (2013): 341–50.

US Department of Health and Human Services. *The Health Consequences of Smoking—50 Years of Progress: A Report of the Surgeon General.* Rockville, MD: US Department of Health and Human Services, 2014.

Chapter 8

American Academy of Child and Adolescent Psychiatry. "Depression in Children and Teens." Accessed February 9, 2018. https://www.aacap.org/AACAP/Families_and_youth/Facts_for_Families/FFF-Guide/The-Depressed-Child-004.aspx.

Bailey, Rahn K., and Dion L. Owens. "Overcoming Challenges in the Diagnosis and Treatment of Attention-Deficit/Hyperactivity Disorder in African Americans." *Journal of the National Medical Association* 97, suppl. 10 (2005): 5S–10S.

Banerjee, Tania Das, Frank Middleton, and Stephen V. Faraone. "Environmental Risk Factors for Attention-Deficit Hyperactivity Disorder." *Acta Pædiatrica* 96, no. 9 (2007): 1269–74.

Bell, Carl C. "Lessons Learned from 50 Years of Violence Prevention Activities in the African American Community." *Journal of the National Medical Association* 109, no. 4 (2017): 224–37.

Bell, Carl C., and Radhika Chimata. "Prevalence of Neurodevelopmental Disorders among Low-Income African Americans at a Clinic on Chicago's South Side." *Psychiatric Services* 66, no. 5 (2015): 539–42.

Filipek, Pauline A., Pasquale J. Accardo, Grace T. Baranek, Edwin H. Cook Jr., Geraldine Dawson, Barry Gordon, Judith S. Gravel, et al. "The Screening and Diagnosis of Autistic Spectrum Disorders." *Journal of Autism and Developmental Disorders* 29, no. 6 (1999): 439–84.

Kessler, Ronald C., Wai Tat Chiu, Olga Demler, and Ellen E. Walters. "Prevalence, Severity, and Comorbidity of 12-Month *DSM-IV* Disorders in the National Comorbidity Survey Replication." *Archives of General Psychiatry* 62, no. 6 (2005): 617–27.

Landa, Rebecca J. "Diagnosis of Autism Spectrum Disorders in the First 3 Years of Life." *Nature Clinical Practice Neurology* 4, no. 3 (2008): 138–47.

Merikangas, Kathleen Ries, Jian-Ping He, Debra Brody, Prudence W. Fisher, Karen Bourdon, and Doreen S. Koretz. "Prevalence and Treatment of

Mental Disorders among US Children in the 2001–2004 NHANES." *Pediatrics* 125, no. 1 (2010): 75–81.

Porche, Michelle V., Lisa R. Fortuna, Julia Y. Lin, and Margarita Alegria. "Childhood Trauma and Psychiatric Disorders as Correlates of School Dropout in a National Sample of Young Adults." *Child Development* 82, no. 3 (2011): 982–98.

Psych Central. "Separation Anxiety Disorder Symptoms." Steve Bressert. Accessed December 26, 2017. https://psychcentral.com/disorders/separation-anxiety-disorder-symptoms.

Chapter 9

Campbell, Noll L., Malaz Boustani, Kathleen A. Lane, S. Gao, Hugh Hendrie, Babar A. Khan, J. R. Murrell, et al. "Use of Anticholinergics and the Risk of Cognitive Impairment in an African American Population." *Neurology* 75, no. 2 (2010): 152–59.

Carr, David B., Steven Gray, Jack Baty, and John C. Morris. "The Value of Informant versus Individual's Complaints of Memory Impairment in Early Dementia." *Neurology* 55, no. 11 (2000): 1724–26.

Charletta, Dale A., Philip B. Gorelick, Timothy J. Dollear, Sally Freels, and Y. Harris. "CT and MRI Findings among African-Americans with Alzheimer's Disease, Vascular Dementia, and Stroke without Dementia." *Neurology* 45, no. 8 (1995): 1456–61.

Cuijpers, Pim. "Depressive Disorders in Caregivers of Dementia Patients: A Systematic Review." *Aging & Mental Health* 9, no. 4 (2005): 325–30.

Davis, Daniel H. J., Sam T. Creavin, Jennifer L. Y. Yip, Anna H. Noel-Storr, Carol Crayne, and Sarah Cullum. "Montreal Cognitive Assessment for the Diagnosis of Alzheimer's Disease and Other Dementias." *Cochrane Database of Systematic Reviews* (2015): CD010775.

Freidl, W., R. Schmidt, W. J. Stronegger, A. Irmler, B. Reinhart, and M. Koch. "Mini Mental State Examination: Influence of Sociodemographic, Environmental and Behavioral Factors, and Vascular Risk Factors." *Journal of Clinical Epidemiology* 49, no. 1 (1996): 73–8.

Graff, Maud J. L., Myrra J. M. Vernooij-Dassen, Marjolein Thijssen, Joost Dekker, Willibrord H. L. Hoefnagels, and Marcel G. M. OldeRikkert. "Effects of Community Occupational Therapy on Quality of Life, Mood, and Health Status in Dementia Patients and Their Caregivers: A Randomized Controlled Trial." *The Journals of Gerontology: Series A* 62, no. 9 (2007): 1002–09.

Kaplan, Harrold, and Benjamin Sadock. "Dementia." In *Synopsis of Psychiatry*, by Benjamin Sadock and Harrold Kaplan, 328. Baltimore: Lipincott, Williams & Wilkins, 1998.

Petersen, Ronald C., G. E. Smith, Emre Kokmen, Robert J. Ivnik, and Eric G. Tangalos. "Memory Function in Normal Aging." *Neurology* 42, no. 2 (1992): 396.

Schulz, Richard, Steven H. Belle, Sara J. Czaja, Kathleen A. McGinnis, Alan Stevens, and Song Zhang. "Long-Term Care Placement of Dementia Patients and Caregiver Health and Well-Being." *Journal of the American Medical Association* 292, no. 8 (2004): 961–67.

Thomas, Philippe, Fabrice Lalloué, Pierre-Marie Preux, Cyril Hazif-Thomas, Sylvie Pariel, Robcis Inscale, Joël Belmin, and Jean-Pierre Clément. "Dementia Patients Caregivers Quality of Life: The PIXEL Study." *International Journal of Geriatric Psychiatry* 21, no. 1 (2006): 50–6.

UpToDate. "Evaluation of Cognitive Impairment and Dementia." Eric Larson. Last updated September 20, 2017. https://www.uptodate.com/contents/evaluation-of-cognitive-impairment-and-dementia.

Chapter 10

Dulcan, Mina K. *Helping Parents, Youth, and Teachers Understand Medications for Behavioral and Emotional Problems: A Resource Book of Medication Information Handouts*. 3rd ed. Washington, DC: American Psychiatric Association, 2007.

MedlinePlus Medical Encyclopedia. "Serotonin Syndrome." Last updated December 21, 2017. https://medlineplus.gov/ency/article/007272.htm.

Sadock, Benjamin J., Virginia A. Sadock, and Pedro Ruiz. *Kaplan & Sadock's Synopsis of Psychiatry: Behavioral Sciences/Clinical Psychiatry*. 11th ed. Philadelphia: Wolters Kluwer, 2015.

Chapter 11

Arkowitz, Hal, and Scott O. Lilienfeld. "Is Mindfulness Good Medicine?" *Scientific American* 5, no. 25 (2014): 74–5.

Kerner, Nancy, and Joan Prudic. "Current Electroconvulsive Therapy Practice and Research in the Geriatric Population." *Neuropsychiatry* 4, no. 1 (2014): 33–54.

Larson, David B., Kimberly A. Sherrill, John S. Lyons, Frederic C. Craigie Jr., Samuel B. Thielman, Mary A. Greenwold, and Susan S. Larson. "Associations between Dimensions of Religious Commitment and Mental Health Reported in the *American Journal of Psychiatry* and *Archives of General Psychiatry*: 1978–1989." *American Journal of Psychiatry* 149, no. 4 (1992): 557–59.

Linde, Klaus, Gilbert Ramirez, Cynthia D. Mulrow, Andrej Pauls, Wolfgang Weidenhammer, and Dieter Melchart. "St John's Wort for Depression—An

Overview and Meta-Analysis of Randomised Clinical Trials." *BMJ* 313, no. 7052 (1996): 253–58.

Logan, Alan C. "Omega-3 Fatty Acids and Major Depression: A Primer for the Mental Health Professional." *Lipids in Health and Disease* 3, no. 1 (2004): 25.

Miller, Laura J. "Use of Electroconvulsive Therapy during Pregnancy." *Psychiatric Services* 45, no. 5 (1994): 444–50.

Weir, Kirsten. "The Exercise Effect." *Monitor on Psychology* 42, no. 11 (2011): 48.

Chapter 12

Atdjian, Sylvia, and William A. Vega. "Disparities in Mental Health Treatment in US Racial and Ethnic Minority Groups: Implications for Psychiatrists." *Psychiatric Services* 56, no. 12 (2005): 1600–02.

Berkeley, Malaika E. "Patient 24." In *Psychiatry Pearls*, by Alex Kolevzon and Daniel G. Stewart, 83–7. Philadelphia: Hanley & Belfus, 2004.

Bureau of Justice Statistics. "Estimated Number of Sentenced Prisoners under State and Federal Jurisdiction, by Sex, Race, Hispanic Origin, and Age." Accessed January 13, 2018. https://www.bjs.gov/index.cfm?ty=nps.

Henry J. Kaiser Family Foundation. "Disparities in Health and Health Care: Five Key Questions and Answers." Petry Ubri and Samantha Artiga. Accessed January 29, 2017. http://kff.org/disparities-policy/issue-brief/disparities-in-health-and-health-care-five-key-questions-and-answers/.

Institute of Medicine. *Unequal Treatment: Confronting Racial and Ethnic Disparities in Health Care.* Washington, DC: The National Academies Press, 2003.

National Institute of Health and US Department of Health and Human Services. "NIH Health Disparities Strategic Plan, Fiscal Years 2004–2008,

Volume 1." Accessed February 8, 2018. https://www.nimhd.nih.gov/docs/2004_2008_strategic_plan_vol1.pdf.

National Institutes of Mental Health. "Closing the Gaps: Reducing Disparities in Mental Health Treatment through Engagement." Accessed January 29, 2017. https://www.nimh.nih.gov/research-priorities/scientific-meetings/2011/closing-the-gaps-reducing-disparities-in-mental-health-treatment-through-engagement/index.shtml.

Oxford English Dictionary. "Racism." Accessed January 29, 2017. http://www.oed.com.

Snowden, Lonnie R. "Bias in Mental Health Assessment and Intervention: Theory and Evidence." American Journal of Public Health 93, no. 2 (2003): 239–43.

Sourcebook of Criminal Justice Statistics. "Juveniles in Public and Private Residential Custody Facilities, by Race, Ethnicity, and Offense, United States." Accessed January 13, 2008. https://www.albany.edu/source-book/tost_6.html#6_b.

University of Minnesota. "Causes of Health Disparities." Accessed January 29, 2017. http://www.epi.umn.edu/let/nutri/disparities/causes.shtm.

US Department of Health and Human Services. Mental Health: Culture, Race, and Ethnicity—A Supplement to Mental Health: A Report of the Surgeon General. Rockville, MD: US Department of Health and Human Services, 2001.

ABOUT THE AUTHORS

Otis Anderson III, MD

Dr. Otis Anderson III is a community psychiatrist practicing in the state of Mississippi. He is currently the sole psychiatrist at First Counseling in Southaven. He is a former correctional psychiatrist for the state prison system in Mississippi. He is a rural mental health champion as one of six outpatient Medicaid providers for children in the whole state of Mississippi. He also serves as the medical director for the chemical dependency unit at Tri-Lakes Hospital in Batesville and does some psychiatric consulting for various senior care units in northern Mississippi.

He is a former Substance Abuse and Mental Health Services Administration fellow for the American Psychological Association (APA) and also held a position on the APA's board of representatives in 2008–2009. He served as the member-in-training representative to the Black Psychiatrists of America's board of trustees from 2008 to 2010. He is currently active in his Memphis community and serves on the board of directors for Memphis Challenge, an organization founded by AutoZone to promote education and leadership development in Memphis's "talented tenth" youth.

Dr. Anderson believes that "no matter what your age, from four to one hundred four, and no matter where your judgment takes you, from your city or town to substance abuse recovery and incarceration and back into the community, Dr. Anderson will come see ya! Mental health matters to me!"

Timothy G. Benson, MD

Dr. Timothy G. Benson is a Harvard-trained psychiatrist double-boarded in psychiatry and addiction medicine. He is also the author of the book *Surviving Success*.

Dr. Benson completed his medical degree at the University of Rochester School of Medicine and his adult psychiatry residency at Harvard Medical School's Massachusetts General Hospital/McLean Hospital. He also served as medical director of the McLean Center at Fernside, a nationally acclaimed residential addiction facility. As a sports and addiction psychiatrist, Dr. Benson has served as a consultant to both the NBA and the NFL.

In addition to his clinical work, Dr. Benson is passionate about giving back. He speaks nationally to high schools, colleges, and athletic teams on the topics of "Succeeding against the Odds" and "Surviving Success: Performing under the Pressures of High Expectations."

Dr. Benson practices in the Los Angeles metropolitan area. Providing both psychotherapy and medication management, he treats depression, anxiety, addiction, and a range of other mental health conditions.

"I am passionate about using my expertise to help individuals maximize their health, relationships, and careers. I learned early in my journey the importance of asking for help even before you think you need it. Knowing that one healthy relationship can make all the difference, it is true that we may go faster alone, but we can go much further together."

Malaika E. Berkeley, MD, MPH

Dr. Malaika Berkeley has traveled a long way from her roots in the South American nation of Guyana and the island of Barbados. She attended the University of Virginia for her undergraduate studies then went on to achieve her Doctor of Medicine degree from Howard University College of Medicine. While pursuing her residency in Psychiatry at Mount Sinai Hospital in New York, Dr. Berkeley was presented with the Women Leaders in Psychiatry award.

Following her Residency, Dr. Berkeley worked for many years in a variety of settings focused mainly on the underserved population. She has worked at community hospitals and clinics, state hospitals, forensic hospitals, and the prison system. In 2012 Dr. Berkeley received her Master of Public Health from Emory University with a focus on Healthcare Management before opening her private practice. Dr. Berkeley is board certified in General Psychiatry by the American Board of Psychiatry and Neurology. She currently splits her time between her private practice and providing care in various community settings.

Delane Casiano, MD
Treasurer, Global Health Psychiatry

Dr. Delane Casiano is a board-certified adult psychiatrist in Philadelphia, Pennsylvania. With specializations in cultural psychiatry and women's mental health, Dr. Casiano has worked with ethnically diverse populations in a multitude of health care settings. Through her work she is helping individuals overcome challenges with depression and other mental health problems. Dr. Casiano earned her bachelor's degree from Brown University and medical degree from Morehouse School of Medicine. She spent ten years at the Hospital of the University of Pennsylvania where she completed her residency and postdoctoral research training and then served as clinical associate and cultural psychiatry course director.

Professional and governmental organizations such as the American Psychiatric Association and the National Institute of Mental Health have recognized her research examining cultural influences on mental health beliefs among African American men and women with depression. Clinical organizations herald Dr. Casiano's work as well. She collaborated with the Philadelphia Department of Behavioral Health to create a combined program of psychiatry and obstetrics/gynecology services for women. Additionally, she supervised multidisciplinary teams as associate medical director for the Princeton House Behavioral Health women's program.

Dr. Casiano provides academic presentations and educational events for health-care professionals and community members. She continues to see patients in local community mental health centers and in her own private practice in Erdenheim, a nearby Philadelphia suburb.

Ericka Goodwin, MD
President, Global Health Psychiatry

Dr. Ericka Goodwin is a graduate of Spelman College. She completed her MD at Emory University and her general psychiatry residency at Morehouse School of Medicine. After serving as chief resident, Dr. Goodwin became the second American Psychiatric Association Jeanne Spurlock Congressional fellow. She then completed a child and adolescent psychiatry fellowship at Children's Hospital Boston-Harvard University. She has held multiple leadership positions in the American Psychiatric Association. She currently works as a traveling psychiatrist (board certified in child, adolescent, and adult psychiatry).

She is dedicated to providing access to quality services to those who would not ordinarily have access to a psychiatrist with her skill and training. She prides herself on exploring each patient as a total person, physically, mentally, and spiritually. Her goal is to provide thoughtful psychiatric services that are fueled by love. She also has a passion for assisting others with integrating principles of mental wellness into everyday life to maximize their personal happiness and success. She focuses on living a healthy lifestyle so that she can lead by example. She is coauthor of the book *Thinking about Quitting Medicine*, which aids her in helping others align their profession with their purpose.

Napoleon B. Higgins Jr., MD
CEO, Global Health Psychiatry

Dr. Napoleon Higgins is a child, adolescent, and adult psychiatrist in Houston, Texas. He is the owner of one of the largest multispecialty mental health groups in the fourth largest city in the United States.

Dr. Higgins received his MD from Meharry Medical College, and he completed his residency in adult psychiatry and his fellowship in child and adolescent psychiatry at the University of Texas Medical Branch at Galveston. He is president of the Black Psychiatrists of Greater Houston and past president of the Black Psychiatrists of America and the Caucus of Black Psychiatrists of the American Psychiatric Association.

In addition of being a coauthor of this book, Dr. Higgins is also author of *Transition 2 Practice*, which encompasses physician practice issues. He specializes in natural health and nutrition to improve patients' lives mentally and physically. He emphasizes that good mental and physical health are key in the practice of psychiatry and medicine. Dr. Higgins has worked with countless inner-city and community mentoring programs. He has special interest in trauma and racism and how they affect minority and disadvantaged children and communities.

James Lee Jr., MD
Secretary, Global Health Psychiatry

Dr. James Lee Jr. is the president/CEO of Ascension Behavioral Healthcare in Rock Hill, South Carolina. He has been in private practice for ten years, specializing in general adult psychiatry. He is a graduate of Morehouse College and Meharry Medical College. After graduating from medical school, he completed his residency in general adult psychiatry at the University of South Carolina/Palmetto Health Alliance. He later completed a fellowship in forensic psychiatry at Tulane University.

Currently, in addition to being in private practice, he serves as medical director for Standards-Based Solutions, a mental health agency in Chapel Hill, North Carolina. He also serves on the faculty of Edward C. Via Osteopathic School of Medicine as an associate professor in the department of psychiatry and as a contract psychiatrist for Winthrop University. Dr. Lee is board certified, and since 2013, he has been a credentialed provider for Transcranial Magnetic Stimulation (TMS), an FDA-approved treatment for depression since 2008.

Michael Pratts, MD

Dr. Michael Pratts is the medical director for Cayuga County Mental Health Center in Auburn, New York. Formerly the medical director of the Comprehensive Psychiatric Emergency Program (CPEP) at St. Joseph's Hospital in Syracuse and director of research at the PANSS Institute, Dr. Pratts received his medical degree from the University of Southern California, completed his adult psychiatry residency at Albert Einstein College of Medicine / Bronx Psychiatric Center, and completed his fellowship training in child and adolescent psychiatry at SUNY Downstate Medical Center. Dr. Pratts is published in major medical journals, including the *New England Journal of Medicine* and the *Journal of Emergency Medicine*. Dr. Pratts is board certified in psychiatry.

Karriem L. Salaam, MD

Dr. Karriem L. Salaam is a board certified adult, child, and adolescent psychiatrist in Philadelphia, Pennsylvania. He is the medical director of the adolescent unit of Friends Hospital, which is the oldest private psychiatric hospital in continuous existence in the United States. He is a clinical assistant professor of psychiatry at Drexel University College of Medicine. Dr. Salaam earned his medical degree from Robert Wood Johnson Medical School. He completed his residency in general psychiatry at Temple University Hospital, where he served as one of the chief residents, and his fellowship in child and adolescent psychiatry at Thomas Jefferson University Hospital, both in Philadelphia. Dr. Salaam is a fellow of the American Psychiatric Association and a member of both the Black Psychiatrists of America and the Caucus of Black Psychiatrists of the American Psychiatric Association. He has special interests in academic achievement among children of color and the relationship between spirituality and mental health.

Teo-Carlo Straun, MD

Dr. Straun is a dedicated medical professional with a wide-ranging skill set suitable for individuals seeking anything from general care to state-of-the-art, evidence-based treatment.

Dr. Straun received his medical degree from Rutgers Medical School, and he completed his residency in adult psychiatry at the University of Medicine and Dentistry. He then completed his fellowship in addiction psychiatry at Yale School of Medicine and currently serves as an assistant professor in psychiatry.

Dr. Straun's professional passion rests in connecting with patients and communities to maximize individuals' mental health and wellness. He is the owner of Straun Health and Wellness, an integrative psychiatric practice focused on mental, physical, and spiritual health, with offices in Connecticut and Massachusetts. Dr. Straun firmly believes that the promotion of mental health and the integration of physical and mental wellness are important factors in determining one's quality of life. His primary modes of service include psychiatric evaluation, a complementary style of psychotherapy, medical management, motivational enhancement therapy, auricular acupuncture, and other holistic models of recovery for individuals suffering from mental illness and substance use disorders. He is a pivotal member of the Barbershop Health Network, a community service project with a mission of decreasing health disparities for men of color using barbers.

Contact information for the authors, all of whom make up Global Health Psychiatry:

Global Health Psychiatry
Website: GHPsychiatry.com
E-mail: info@GHPsychiatry.com
Facebook/Instagram/LinkedIn/Twitter: @GHPsychiatry

Made in the USA
Columbia, SC
25 May 2018